# Whispers of the Underworld

## The Red-light District in Bisbee, Arizona

Richard W. Graeme IV

Dedicated to

Carrie Bush, Ethel Patterson, Rita Reese, Bridget Gallagher & Clara Dodge

May they find happiness unattained in life.

Revised May 18, 2025

# Table of Contents

Introduction -------------------- 4

Restricting the girls ---------- 6

The Ladies --------------------- 35

Denizens of the Underworld- 45

Dens of Dreams --------------- 72

Women Enslaved ------------- 91

Bisbee's Captivatingly Wild Daughters - 101

Vagrants, Miners, Customer Lawmen Fools, and other Ornery Characters ------ 138

Appendix ---------------------------------- 176

Bibliography ------------------------------ 242

# Introduction

Vestiges of the red-light district are found in a steep-walled almost claustrophobic section of Upper Brewery Gulch. The broken foundations of the ill-famed houses survive as low yellowish-rock walls. These are mixed with short staircases of grey, crumbling concrete. It is difficult to imagine that these 400 feet of gulch was home to one of the most turbulent locations of the southwest. Under the light of lanterns, fiery, temperamental, yet scantily–clad ladies tantalized customers from wide porches. The strong notes played from the ivory keys of pianos were accompanied by sweet feminine voices and those deeper sounds of intoxicated miners. Hidden away were smoke filled rooms and intricate oriental pipes, where others found solace in a poppy induced dreamy state. Tempers flared, blood was drawn and life was taken among these ruins. Thieves and brutally mean men called this area home. At the same time these now vacant lots once provided a source for secret desires, passion, infatuation and more rarely true love. Dark rumors slowly developed accusing red-light house owners of participating in the *"White Slave Trade"* and importing sweet, innocent young girls into the wickedness of the red-light life. Then suddenly, with World War I, it was gone. Time eroded, rapidly and harshly at the district's history. Only faint whispers remain of a district whose vitality drove the carnal desires of men wild and filled the purses of alluring goddesses of sex with gold.

A French postcard with a scantily clad lady. c-1907

# The Restricted District

It is unknown when the first dusty, desert dove made her way into the lonely mountains of Bisbee. Concealed within her femininity was the undaunted, steel, courage that matched any prospector, Indian scout or soldier. She would have discovered a camp built of tents and simple wooden and stone houses nestled at the foot of a prominent, red, iron oxide-stained mountain. The simple homes extended up into the narrow grey limestone canyons filled with scrub oak. Acrid smoke from the crude smelter choked the air. Single, youthful, men often of a rather coarse character populated the infant community. The majority worked as miners for the Copper Queen Mining Company or the Holbrook & Cave Mining Company.

For the lady of the bawdy life, Bisbee placed no restrictions on her, she could work or live where she desired. Even saloons initially catered to these adventurous women as well as men. As the mines found increasing amounts of copper ore, it became apparent that Bisbee was not going to be a boom town, but rather a permanent community. Changes began. Other daring women arrived and families immigrated to the obscure little camp. Civilization began. The residents decided that that both the saloons and houses of ill-fame needed to be contained separated from the ideally wholesome homes of families. Thus, began the development of a respectable community. On May 7, 1892, the far end of Brewery Gulch was designated as the red-light district. Locally, the red-light district was often referred to as the "Reservation".

How the earliest ill-famed ladies behaved when they were allowed to work freely among the entire city is unknown, but if the later history gives a clue, creating a restricted district was an excellent decision. These girls and their customers could be mighty wild. In the new red-light district, the girls ideally, would be let to their own vices of uninhibited dancing, gambling, a river of overpriced liquor and more discreetly sex. Those who chose could limit interaction with the decadent ladies by their distance from the district. Details about the early district are few, but as the late 1890's approached, local newspapers had developed. The news of troubles in the red-light district began to be regularly recorded. Generally, they were the same issues that prevailed in all the ill-famed districts in the West, fighting, robbery and drunkenness.

A hefty, monthly license was charged for ill-famed houses in 1902 of $30.00. In 1906, the fees became more specific.

*Houses with four or less girls working at them paid $30.00 a month.*

*Houses with five girls employed were charged $35.00 per month*

*Houses with six ladies were charged $40.00 per month.*

*Houses with seven girls were charged $45.00 per month*

*Houses employing eight girls paid $50.00 per month*

*Any house were more than eight girls were employed paid $60.00 per month*

Over two dozen brothels that operated in Bisbee and surrounding communities.

**Brewery Gulch**

Julius Cardinas Place, (1897)

Anita Romero's House, (1899-1901)

"Mexican Dance Hall", (1899)

Canadian Club, (1909)

Casino, (1909)

Cora Miles House, (1902- 1907)

Cribs houses no. 100- 145 (not house numbers), (1908)

Hog Ranch/ Coon Joint, Mrs. Mary Geary, (1897- 1901)

Hog Ranch, Emma Voeltzel (1902)

Helen McHenry's House, (1907)

Little Casino, (1909) (Note, there was also a Little Casino Saloon on Main Street in 1906)

Little Club, (1904-1909)

"Manicure Parlor" run by N.M. Petty, (1910)

Majestic, (1912)

Mascot, (1908)

No. 9, (1909)

No. 10 (1902)

No. 33, (1909)

No.41 (may be the same as No.128), (1909)

No.48, (1902)

No. 114 operated by Nellie Wright, (1909)

No. 128 run by Jack Kerner, (1908)

People's Theater, (1906) operated by Barney Echstein

Rose Miller's Place, (1901)

Ruby-Glim Row, (1909-1910)

Shea House, (1905)

**Johnson Addition**

Riverside Park / Beer Garden, (1909)

**Lowell Houses**

Upper Lowell Club, (1914)

Shea House, (1907)

**Illegally run houses out of district**

Opera Club (Tombstone Canyon/ Main Street), (1903)

Norton House Tombstone Canyon/ Main Street, (1906)

**Tintown**

Unidentified House, (1910)

French postcard c-1907

View of Brewery Gulch from Queen Hill with red-light district indicated. c-1914

Bisbee's red-light district c-1910. This is one of three known photographs of the active district.

In 1902, laws were also passed that prohibited women from entering saloons outside of the red-light district. This was to prevent the girls from procuring customers outside the ill-famed district and prevent young girls from being influenced and joining the ill-famed lifestyle. At the same time children were forbidden from being in an ill-famed house between 9:00 pm and 6:00 am without a legitimate excuse. In modern times it may confusing to think children were allowed at all in the red-light district, until one remembers that underage boys performed essential work in the community by delivering groceries, purchased dry goods, newspapers and messages. This system did not work perfectly. In 1905, William Phillips a seventeen-year-old was stabbed to death in a fight at the Little Casino, a red-light house. The fight started over one of the district's girls. One young newspaper boy discovered an attractive recent addition to the district and arranged for a short time to trade the newspaper for her services.

A delivery wagon at the mouth of O.K. Street with a young boy reaching up to the awning. c-1908.

During 1905, laws were drawn up creating two saloon districts One on Main Street, south of Castle Rock and another in Brewery Gulch from the mouth until the city limits. The saloons were required to be operated within 200 ft. of the streets. Saloons were still allowed inside the red-light district.

Ill-famed houses were not the only buildings in the red-light district. There were regular homes located above the gulch bottom and away from the ill-famed houses and further up the gulch in an area known as Zacatecas Canyon. The Queen Laundry was an important business legally located in the gulch beyond the houses of the red-light district. At times the residents living in the district would become annoyed with their loud neighbors as regular citizens still lived there until its closure and beyond.

Many a customer of the district found their wallet suffering from a lack of currency after a visit. It can be argued that in many cases the men were too drunk to remember spending their money. In other cases the ladies provided a convenient explanation or scapegoat to explain missing cash. Of course, some of the men were actually robbed. Regardless, being robbed in the districts became a symbol of a young man's foolishness.

Right: A mass produced comic stereo view depicting a woman robbing a sleeping man. c -1900

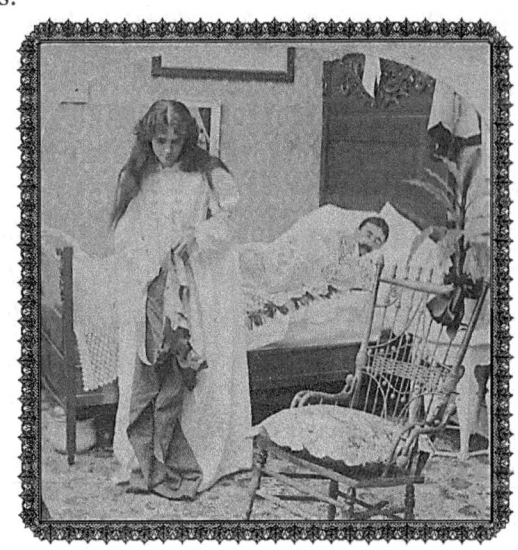

Brawls were common, often these were simply just two men settling their problems with fists. Yet, others chose the deadliness of a thin steel blade or the cocking of a cold steel pistol. On April 27, 1907, red-light madam, Lee Watson was confronted by one of her girls, Rosie Highwarton. Rosie's consort Harry Highwarton grabbed and held Lee while Rosie's proceeded to stab her with a knife. Watson was seriously, but not fatally injured. The Highwartons were held for a Grand Jury. There was indication that this attack may have been revenge for an undescribed incident in Montana in 1902. Because of such incidents, a special duty night police officers had to be assigned to restrain the ladies and men of the district.

At times, the occupants of different houses would battle each other leaving the ground covered in shattered glass. The justice court would be filled with red-light girls and their consorts. These girls entered the court dressed in the peaks of fashion and wearing a few battle wounds. Such an event was recorded in 1912.

*"The Majestic, a resort in the reservation, was scene of a three hour battle early yesterday morning, in which bottles glasses and fist were used to detriment of heads and furniture. The Fight, which raged with varying intensity, followed a post-pay day revelry. It began about 4 o'clock and the din of battle did not die until the limpid light of seven o'clock in the morning lit up the ghastly, glass-strewn battle ground.*

*With the exception of black eyes, red noses, green snakes and brown tastes, no damage was done to the participants, including Amazons of the Underworld, silk-socked hangers-on and invaders of the reservation. The fight was all local as the battle of Agua Prieta or the siege of Naco and reports of the fight did not reach the police until after the empty bottle ammunition gave out and the fighting ceased.*

*A piano that had been rented was ruined by a flood of broken glass and wine and the owner compelled the renter to purchase outright, it being fit for nothing but Turkey Trot rag."* (March 13, 1912).

A more unique problem was the girls renting horses. The

ladies were notorious for wildly racing them along Naco Road and sometimes even into the ill-famed district. The Bisbee Daily Review reported these details of the ride that two girls that had rented horses.

At 5; 30 am July 10, 1906, *"thinking a troop of cavalry must be going through town, the curious raised the windows and peering out beheld two daring female riders urging two foam-flecked steeds in a neck to neck race"* The two riders of the red-light were arrested by Officer Jay Wilmoth.

Ada Beaumont was one of these daring ladies until, she was thrown from her horse and fractured both her upper and lower jaw. The injury was predicted to be fatal and the other girls in the district packed her belongings, removing anything that indicated her illicit past and sent her home to Kentucky. It is unknown whether it was truly a fatal injury.

The Palace Livery Stable on Main Street.
It was from livery stables that the ill-famed ladies rented horses. c-1904

A few months earlier, May Derowe a girl from No. 41 was thrown from a horse. The doctors felt that her massive hairdo cushioned the blow and possibly saved her life. It was popular at the time, to add extra hairpieces even to luxuriant natural hair.

A French caricature poking fun at the massive Edwardian hairstyles.
c-1905

Ed Fletcher saw a girl who had rented one of his horses to go to the circus. She was wildly intoxicated and had run the horse into a barbed wire fence. In trying to stop the woman and rescue the injured horse, Frank Haywood a man riding with the scarlet lady, struck him on the neck, leaving Fletcher temporarily unable to speak.

In 1903, mining operations in Bisbee exploded in number and moved south east from Bisbee. As a result, the suburb of Lowell was built. By 1904, the ladies of the red-light began to move into Lowell. At this time, Lowell was considered its own community separate from Bisbee with its own Justice Court and police officers. The vivacious women found themselves unwelcome and were met with resistance, but Con & Lillian Shea successfully moved their house from Brewery Gulch to Upper Lowell.

> I wish to notify the people of Lowell and Bisbee that I am in no way connected with the Lowell Red Light district, as I was in business here when they started up, and am still running my own business.
> LOWELL SALOON,
> Jonathan W. Noel, Prop.

Announcement in Bisbee Daily Review, 1905

Also, the Beer Garden in Johnson Addition at times was frequented by ill-famed ladies. Red-light houses in Lowell were quieter than on Brewery Gulch. One of the few occasions that trouble resulted was when Nellie Bond an ill-famed girl walked through Lowell completely nude and totally intoxicated. On July 16, 1910, at around between 2 and 3 am four women broke out into a brawl that was describe as *"a racket as one might suppose would happen were a good sized cattery to be suddenly dumped into a well populated dog kennel."* Four women were arrested and were referred as *May Coe, Claire Doe, Myrtle Hoe* and *Pearl Roe*. Their actual names are unknown and they were likely girls of the red-light. The exact locations of the houses are unclear, but they were in upper Lowell and Johnson Addition. One short lived ill-famed house operated further south in Tin Town during 1910. Little is known about this house, but the madam was arrested on immigration violations.

Lowell, c-1908

Thoughtful planning of the designers of the Warren community prevented any of the land sold by the Warren Development Company to *"at any time be used for the sale of intoxicating liquors in any form, nor for gambling places or houses of ill-fame: also the must not be used for slaughter-houses, hog-pens or any form of nuisance or approach thereto."* Warren was developed to be *"The City Beautiful"* a planned community where both company officials and miners lived in and away from the socially and physically polluted canyons of Bisbee. No houses of ill-fame are known to have existed in this part of town. A young lady, Carmen Mora was arrested for running completely nude through Warren in 1907. The woman had become intoxicated with Camilo Cortez and Daniel Tapia. Carmen decided she wanted to sprint naked through the areas where houses were to be built. Drunkenly, the two men ran after her. Construction workers and residents of Warren were treated to this entertaining if not shocking sight. All, three were arrested. Carmen received 60 days in jail and the two men were given small fines. Although, Carmen made less than ideal choices, there is no conclusive evidence she was an ill-famed lady.

Along Vista Park in Warren. c-1914

Central School was problematic for the ill-famed district. A small adobe school house had been replaced by a massive multi-storied building in 1905. The structure was located 1,200 ft. from the red-light district's southern boundary. This was the minimum legal distance that the red-light district could be located near a school. In 1906, the minimum legal distance was upped to 1,300 ft. This forced the closure of the ill-famed houses on the southern end of the red-light district.

Central School, c-1908

The girls had difficulty respecting this law and tried to operate their houses even on Main Street. Arrests were made at the Opera Club Lodging House, the Norton House and in the apartments above the Butte Saloon. On the Broadway pathway and near the Calumet and Arizona Hospital, ill-famed ladies also opened houses. At the Butte Saloon, in 1905 the women were accused of trying to attract customers on the street below while scantily clad. Mrs. Fox one of the accused had been seen frequenting wine rooms to solicit customers. She had also been discovered on the streets trying to improve business. Mrs. Fox was arrested and found guilty. Justice McDonald fined her $75.00 and released her after her attorney appealed the conviction. The young lady then proceeded to harass the jurors who found her guilty in the town. The Norton House was particularly problematic. Constables knew the building was being used for immoral purposes. They had investigated, but each time the officers were unable to charge a woman. Finally, in April of 1906, the Norton House was raided and four women were arrested for operating an ill-famed house within 1,300 ft. of Central School. This last raid seemed to quell the interest of ill-famed girls using this building as a place of business.

Norton House on Main Street, c-1904

Painted ladies women were low on society's social scale, but they were not at the bottom. The lowest level was reserved for a despised group that lived in the red-light district as vagrants. Hobos and tramps also passed through the district and often were not overly popular, and were being charged with vagrancy or *"vagged"* to get them to leave town. The true despicable vagrants in the minds of the citizens were men who had no visible income and lived off the earnings of an ill-famed lady. Police constables regularly searched for and arrested individuals in the district on vagrancy charges. Typically, they skipped town before their trial at the justice court, but there was a constant stream of new vagrants to replace them. To help eliminate them in 1914, a law was passed that prohibited any man from working or living at an ill-famed house. This included piano players. The law further stated that men in general were not allowed to be seen in public with the ladies. This was to prevent *"chaste"* women and children from seeing well-dressed men with elegant ill-famed ladies riding together thru town. Bisbee wanted to prevent any encouragement for a young woman to join the life of the red-light.

The wild events of misbehavior built up and over time, it became essential to place further restrictions on the district. On April 1, 1910, Bisbee City Ordinance 153 went into effect and closed all dance halls and saloons in the red-light district. April Fool's Day 1910:

*"Last night marked the final appearance of Bisbee's tenderloin as a blazing myriad of mahogany counters, foaming liquor, polished glasses and "Smiling young man dressed in white." Foolish young swains inflamed by liquor can no longer visit that district and spend what money they have in a wild debauch with the female denizens of the region, paying exorbitant prices for what they drunkenly consume".*

*"Then again, last night the bawdy-house orchestras sounded their farewell notes, the women hopped about in a farewell two-step and the dance hall doors were closed to open no more. The polished floors will either be left deserted or turned into parlor apartments."*

For the girls, this was financially devastating. They depended on dancing and commissions on selling overpriced drinks as an essential part of their income. After this legislation, the district declined and a newspaper claimed that half the girls left for other red-light districts. Particularly, the girls headed for the district at El Paso. The closing of the red-light district's saloons was less effective. Liquor was brought into the district by the customers or *"given away"* by the house. Also in 1910, the girls were ordered to stop advertising in the district by standing outside their rooms scantily dressed, enticing potential customers

The robbing and drunkenness still continued as before, but the Bisbee Daily Review expressed concern that the new restrictions had resulted in a surge of violence. This increase appears to be in inter-house conflicts and resulted from difficulty to earn an adequate income and heightened competition. They were no longer selling companionship by drinking and dancing. The market was largely reduced to sex.

Bisbee was a tolerant community and did even not make a fuss over the X-ray gown that actress Claire Simpson wore through town. Made of diaphanous cloth, the dress exposed more than it concealed. She was later arrested in Tucson for wearing the same outfit. Yet, this toleration had limits.

Bull fighting at nearby Naco, Sonora was poorly received by Bisbee residents. This was largely blamed on the practice of having the bulls gore horses to death before the fight to show their ferocity. This unnecessary blood thirsty feature was highly disapproved of and likely lead to the failure of this form of entertainment. Also, the artist talents of Adolphe Cedro failed to meet public approval in Bisbee. He was known to use the ladies of the underworld for his inspiration and painted them only in the *"habiliments of nature."* An oil painting that he created under commission of Ray Ovens was discovered by the constables during a raid and Adolphe was arrested for painting lewd pictures. Interestingly, the painting seized was painted on the box that once contained a burial robe. During his trial, the painting faced away from the audience and was discreetly shown to the jury members. Although, the arresting officers artist recognized the talent of his technique and use of color, his work of art was taken to Tombstone to be destroyed. The artist was sentence to 90 days in jail without his brushes and paints. Ovens paid three dollars for the painting, but later received a $50.00 fine for distributing a lewd painting.

A French woman wrapped in diaphanous cloth, c-1907

Floods and fires had plagued the community since the early days, but the red-light district was largely spared. There were a few small fires, but these were quickly extinguished. On July 22, 1910, in the height of the *"monsoon season"*, a torrent came down the upper reaches of Zacatecas Canyon tearing apart buildings and damaging others. The Bisbee Daily Review stated,

*"The denizens of this section who were flooded out are housed with their more fortunate neighbors on the high ground while lights left burning reveal the scene of wreck, ruin and disarray of gaudy*

*furniture. At one point where a house was more badly damaged than usual a woman sat on the opposite side of the street in the room of a friend who had taken her in. In her hand she held a Colt's 45, and called a shrill warning to any who ventured too near her ruined house."*

Buildings in Bisbee's red-light district damaged by the 1910 flood
(Courtesy of the Bisbee Mining & Historical Museum)

Another flood in 1917, left the rooms of the girl's knee deep in mud and one ill-famed lady who was sick in bed was rescued only moments before her house was washed away. Many of the district's residents were left with only inadequate clothing. The majority of their clothes being ruined. Early estimates predicted $10,000 of damage to Upper Brewery Gulch not including individual losses.

In 1910, revolution broke out in Mexico. Bisbee residents had strong ties to Mexican communities particularly to Cananea, Sonora. Both communities contained large numbers of former residents of each city. Regiments of soldiers were quickly stationed along

Artillerymen near Naco Arizona. c-1914

the border, including Douglas, and Naco Arizona to protect American interests. A new period of prosperity began for the girls. Thousands of bored, single, young men with steady incomes were now stationed a few miles from Bisbee.

Albeit, battles did occur at Agua Prieta and Naco, Sonora and eventually, Naco, Sonora was under siege for 118 days. Largely, this was a tiresome deployment into the middle of nowhere for most soldiers. Bisbee's saloons and the red-light district were tantalizing attractions.

Yaqui rebels at Naco, Sonora Mexico. c-1913

On January 1, 1915, Arizona became a dry state. The proximity to Mexico provided a supply of alcoholic beverages. By this time, the soldiers were getting into trouble. Soldiers had robbed a couple of red-light girls in Bisbee. Irene Brown was threatened with a straight razor as a tenth cavalry soldier robbed her. At nearby Douglas, Bernard Wilson a member of the Tenth Cavalry was killed protecting a red-light girl on 6th street in Douglas from two other soldiers. Also, the U.S. Army was becoming frustrated with the local law enforcements inability to control illegal alcohol. The U.S. Secretary of War placed the Douglas Red-light District out of bounds for soldiers, but worded it in such a way that it could mean any such district.

In late November 1917, an army officer made a study of the impact of Bisbee's red-light district on the military camps at Lowell, Douglas and Naco. His research revealed that Bisbee's girls often traveled to Douglas and Naco to visit the soldiers. A few weeks later, December 4, 1917, the U.S. Secretary of War sent the City of Bisbee a directive to close the red-light district. The mandate stated that as it was illegal to have an army encampment within five miles of a red-light district. A detachment of the U.S. Army's 35$^{th}$ infantry was camped, below Lowell about two miles from the ill-famed district.

New Jersey National Guard Soldiers in Bisbee's
Red-light District, c-1916 (Courtesy New Jersey State Archives)

Pressured by patriotism, the Bisbee city council guided by Mayor Erickson voted to close the district for the duration of what was to become known as World War I. U.S. Army, Lieutenant Poppaneau attended a Bisbee City Council meeting as a representative of the federal government and thanked the city for its cooperation.

The closure of the legal district came quickly and quietly. The ill-famed ladies left Bisbee on passenger trains for other communities. Each train carried a few of the girls. At 2:00 am. on December 10, 1917, the last legal house of prostitution closed its doors. A few ladies remained waiting to leave and sell the gaudy furniture and other fixtures of the district. In contrast to the days of colorfully written articles of the district. The closure was noted briefly on the last page of the Bisbee Daily Review.

Unofficially, the former district still housed ill-famed ladies. In early 1918, two naive young men went up to the old red-light district to rent a room. They quickly discovered that more than a room was for rent. This led to the arrest of Billie Anderson and her mother Rosa Reed. The reporter for the Bisbee Daily Review found the story of the gullible young men rather amusing. Other women continued to use the former red-light district to conduct their bawdy business for decades after its official closure.

A rental ad for the Mascot a former (?) red-light house.
Bisbee Daily Review April 9, 1918

Yet, nearly a decade before its closure the district was beginning to decline. The original community of single, well-paid miners living in the desolate high desert more than a hundred miles from Tucson and fifty miles from a railroad had been replaced by a thriving city of families with street cars, electricity and a railroad depot in the center of town. More importantly the role of women had changed. Suffrage had been adopted in 1915 by Arizona. A minimum wage law of $10.00 a week for women called the red-light abatement act had been passed in 1917. An increasing number of women were seeking higher education and better employment opportunities were beginning to form.

Empowerment of woman was even expressed in fashion. The binding corset which had forced a lady's figure into the desired shape was replaced by comfortable vertical, free flowing clothes. Stiff high collars and long sleeve gave way to open low curved collars and short sleeves. Significantly more of a woman was now up for show.

Still the ill-famed ladies are an integral part of Bisbee's past. Joe Chisholm one of the men who had experienced the district wrote that *"in the first hectic days of the frontier they were about the only womankind the wild Southwest knew. Perhaps the only kind it could have known."*

French postcard c-1910

Top: Part of the former red-light district in 2016.
Middle: The active red-light district around 1910.
Bottom: A composite of both images showing the placement of main people.

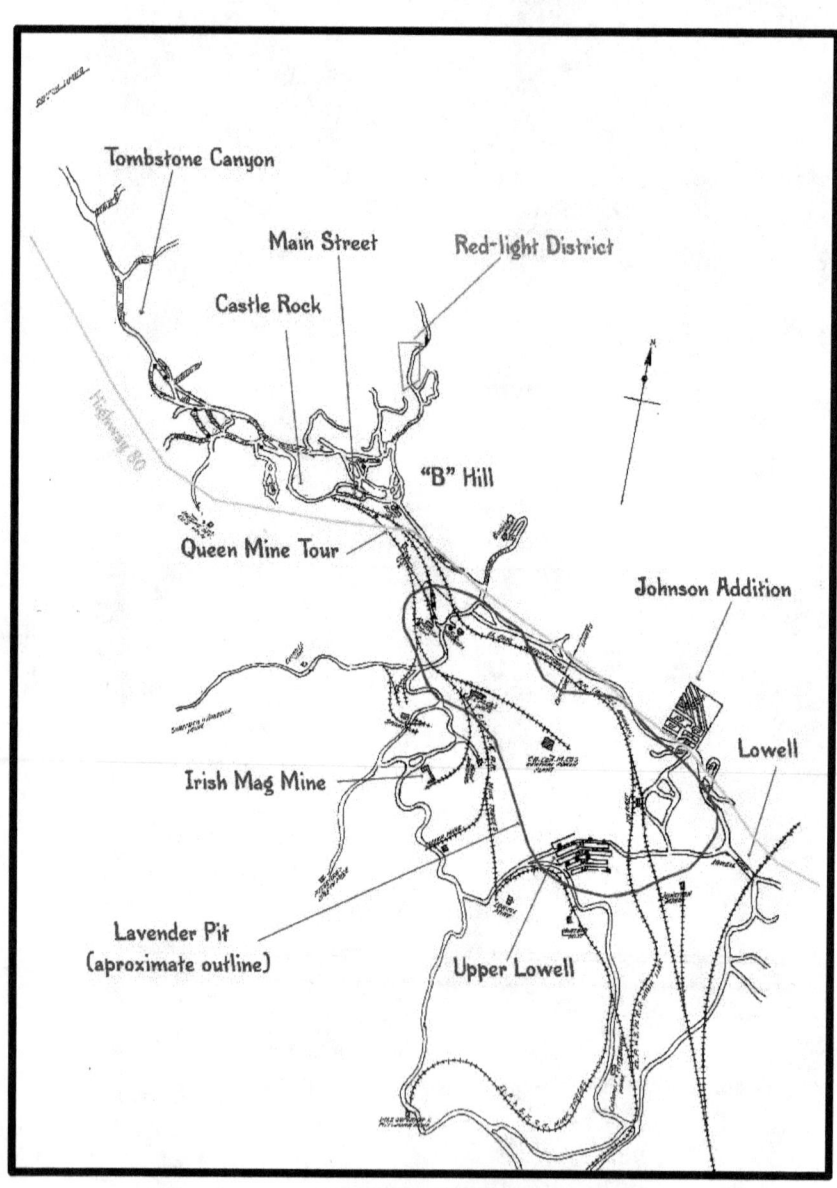

A general map of Bisbee showing the location of the red-light district.

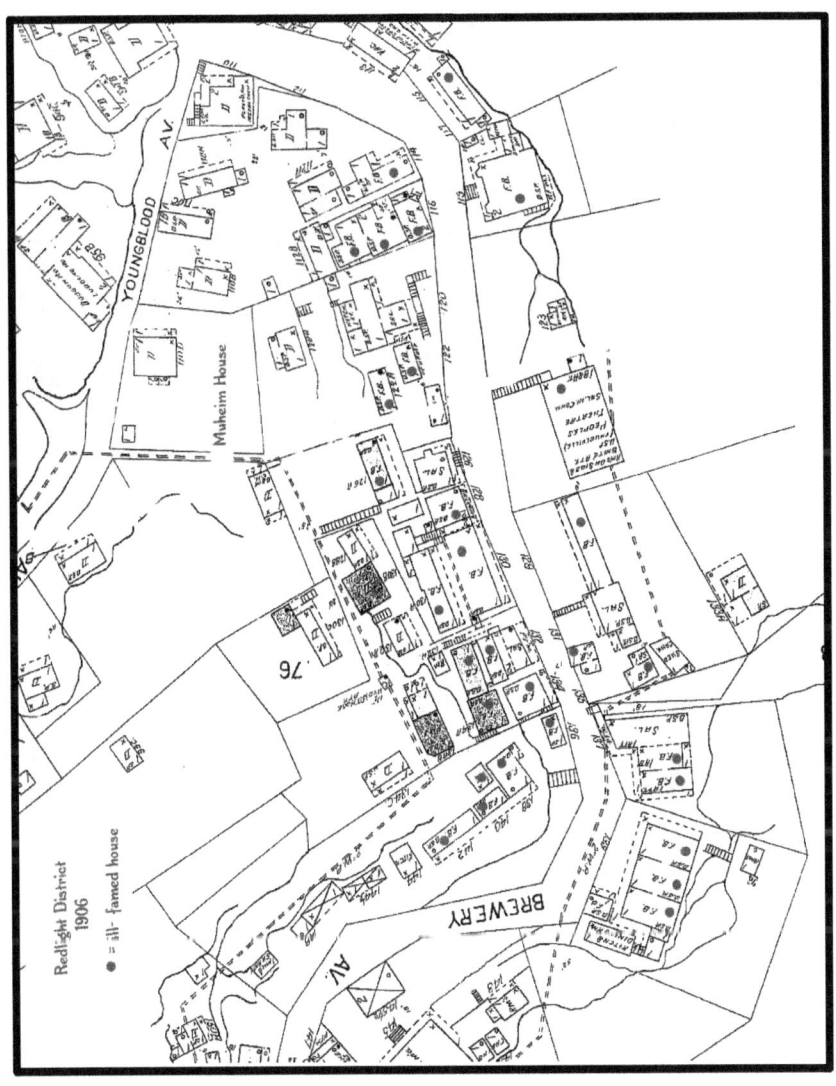

A map showing the known red-light houses active in 1906.

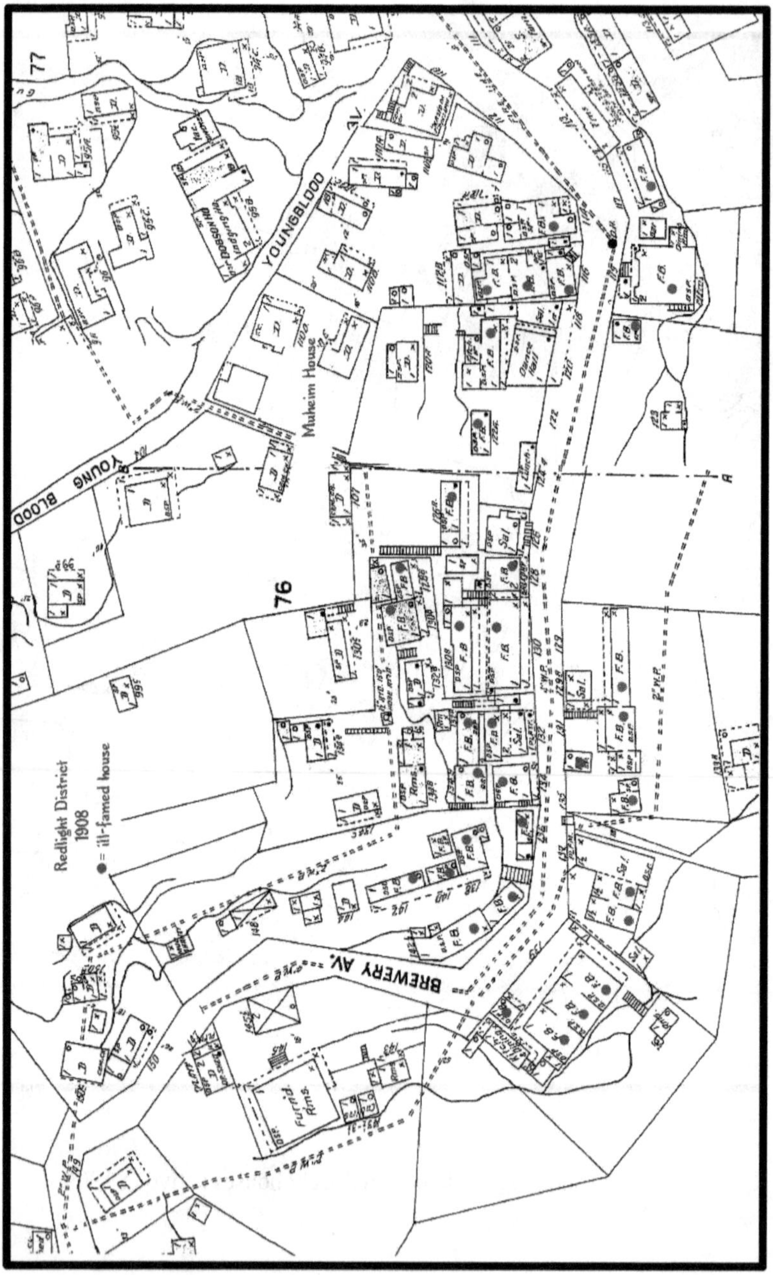

A map showing the location of the red-light houses active in 1908

# The Ladies

These are only known images of women in Bisbee's red-light district while it was active. c-1910

History, normally only recorded the rowdy girls. At times the district was home to nearly 100 ladies, but at any given time only about ten are found in primary documents. These are typically, coroner's reports, newspaper articles and judicial records. This creates a tainted view of their history. The majority of the women seem to have led relatively quiet lives or at least avoided legal troubles. Also, the wonderful and quintessential elements of humanity are normally forgotten. Caring, compassion, kindness and love rarely make history. Yet, a few precious glimpses can be found. In one preserved oral history a woman tells that as a little girl, she remembered the ill-famed ladies purchasing shoes for school children that could not afford them. A coroner's inquest, tells of Ethel Patterson carefully purchasing an outfit of clothes for her son who lived with her parents in the last hours of her life. Even the "wild little animal" Anita Romero is recorded as proudly telling of how her eldest daughter was graduating from high school and would grow up to be a lady.

Money was the largest reason a woman entered the ill-famed life. During 1905, a woman in Arizona could expect to receive about $1.55 for a day's wages. Miners in Bisbee at this time, received $3.75-$4.00 per day. A woman could not expect to earn a living wage as a clerk or waitress. It was expected that she would be dependent on a husband. Teachers were better paid, but required special training and still would have made substantially less than a miner. In 1907, Arizona's teachers made on average $71.10 a month and at the time they were the highest paid teachers in the United States. An underground miner made between $83 and $96, a month. Note, that Bisbee miners were considered the highest paid in the world at this time. It is important to note that these high wages resulted in a relatively high cost of living, thereby putting an additional financial strain on single women who worked outside of the red-light district.

> **WANTED.**
> WANTED—Immediately, woman for housework, $20 per month. 81 Upper Lowell.        387

Bisbee Daily Review January 1, 1908

As a lady of the night, they could make substantially more income. For sexual services they charged a fee from $ 2.00 and continued up to $10.00, if the customer stayed the night. She also, may receive tips a grateful client left. The exact knowledge of income they made on selling drinks and dancing has become lost to time, but was significant. Although, some girls made enough money to purchase diamonds and other fine jewelry, others like Rita Reese were desperately poor. The elite ill-famed houses that catered to wealthy customers seem to have never developed in Bisbee. Photographs of the district reveal it was built of rather modest wood and sheet metal buildings. It is unknown whether specific girls were able to develop a wealthy clientele.

Women came to the ill-famed life by many routes. Some came to escape poverty, others to flee an unhappy or abusive marriage. Still others were forced into the profession by husbands, siblings or even parents. The youngest documented was a 13-year-old girl with flaming, red, hair. Her parents had forced her into the profession, but she later found a level of respectability when she married Emmett Walsh. Mr. Walsh knew of her past but accepted her and actually even gently teased his wife about her illicit past. *"Slivers"* Glover appears to have been forcing a woman to work in the district. He was arrested after a police officer heard rumors that he had told people that he was planning to *"beat her head off"* if she had not made any money. The officer reached the house in the district, just as he was releasing a barrage of verbal abuse on the girl. Felix Taylor was arrested for prostituting his own wife, Harriet. Wife of a popular miner, Mrs. Kathryn Mabry was arrested for trying to lure underage girls into the immoral lifestyle. She offered three young girls an oyster and chicken supper at a home on Naco Road. Mrs. Mabry made great efforts to keep the girls at the house for the entire night. The Bisbee Daily Review reported the young girls even smoked opium. Although, the girls left against the wishes of Mrs. Mabry and did not spend the night, Mrs. Mabry was arrested. At her trial, Mrs. Mabry *"wore an air of defiance",* but she was "clad *in a black skirt and white waist, a black peach basket hat, trimmed with red cherries, set, off her far from bad looks and made her quite a "stunning" figure."* Mrs. Mabry was convicted of her crime.

About the same, Bisbee was again in an uproar when 16-year-old Lillie Neatherlin was discovered working at No.41. It appears that Lillian and definitely, her sister Della had entered the district of their own free will. Accusations were made that the madam of the house, Mrs. Andy Miller refused to let her leave and she was charging with luring an underage girl into an ill-famed life. The case was dismissed because *"the cordina (sic) of the girls themselves shows that they were not of previous chaste character and the charge is not sustainable under the express provision of the statue."*

Underage girls were the exception, most of the ill-famed ladies were from 19-30 years old. Madams were sometimes older, but not necessarily. Anita Romero ran a house when she was 25. Interestingly, the ladies of African descent seem to have been much older. They were typically in their middle thirties.

The girls often adopted alias, nicknames or professional names. For girls like Trixy Fawcett, Lily Silver and Crazy Horse Lil these names became their real names and are found on all official records. Carrie Bush whose actual name has never been discovered was even buried under her alias.

For some like Anita Romero, Ma Reilly, and Crazy Horse Lil the ill-famed lifestyle was a perfect fit. They thrived in the environment. Crazy Horse Lil is described as *"immoral as hell and not a cockeyed bit ashamed of it"* and Anita Romero as *"an animal of the wild."* Others, like Carrie Bush, Rita Reese and Ethel Patterson were trapped in a lifestyle that led only to unhappiness. Yet, it is noted that the girls of the red-light were to be found in all the varieties and personalities of their chaste sisters.

Although, the majority of the ladies were American born, the district did have its share of sturdy Irish girls like May Gillis and Bridget Gallagher. These blended with the French such as Lily Silver or Marguerite Lefebvre, and the German, Marie Happe. Dark-eyed Mexican beauties formed part of the district's population as did a large number of ebony ladies of African descent. Rosie Highwarton claimed to be partly Native American. The district lacked the presence of any Oriental beauties.

The German risqué actress Mary Irber. c-1908

A French/German young lady c. 1907

Period risqué postcard images of

Right: A Mexican lady draped in a flag c-1907

Below right: A young American beauty-1907

Below left: An alluring French-African woman. C-1910

In 1907, the Bisbee Daily Review noted there was an unwritten law than people of Asian descent could not live in Bisbee. Local legend states that this was because Chinese would open laundries and this was one of the few respectable jobs a single woman could hold. As a result, it was said a Chinese could not stay the night in Bisbee. Exceptions were made for respectable citizens. A number of Japanese engineers were frequent guests of the Copper Queen Consolidated Mining Company from 1900-1917. A Japanese mining engineer, Takeo Shikamura was hired by the Copper Queen and his family did reside in Bisbee from 1909 to at least 1918. For a taste of the Orient, a man would have to travel to the red-light districts a few miles south in Mexico. These districts did employee Asian girls.

Fashion was all important in the district. It was an essential element to the ill-famed business and a times competition was fierce. The earliest scarlet ladies are noted to have observed any ladies arriving to Bisbee to inspect the new fashions popular in the metropolitan areas in the East. The district reached its peak during the early Edwardian period and the *"Gibson Girl"* look was all the rage. A trial at the Justice Court was another reason to dress up in finery and flaunt it to the citizens. *"Justice Murphy's court room was transformed yesterday into what at first looked like an advertisement for a ladies' tailor shop. There were loud green suits, creations of dazzling purple and scarlet, with picture hats to match, suits of conventional black and flaming red. The air was heavily perfumed and paint and powder added luminous luster to the countances (sic) of those ensconced beneath the huge millinery creations"*

After 1888, when the railroad came to Bisbee and modern fashions were readily available at both the Copper Queen and Fair Stores. These stores prided themselves in stocking high quality fashionable merchandise.

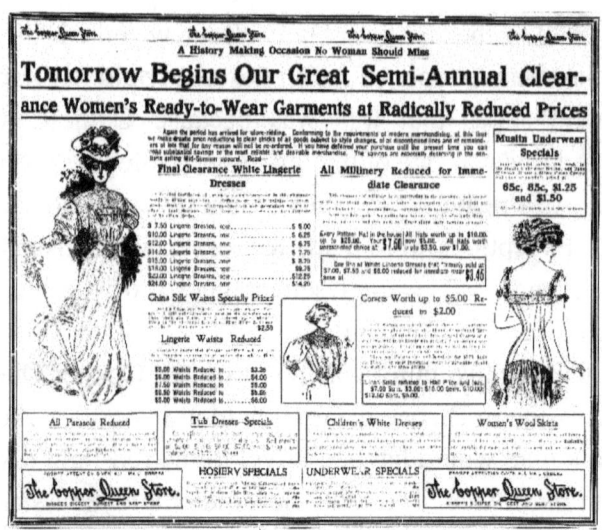

Copper Queen Store Advertisement July 12, 1908

Window display of women's clothing at the Copper Queen Store on Main Street.
c-1914

Religion was not entirely forsaken by the ladies. Although, they may have not been among the Sunday church going group, they at least maintained a connection. Hospital records reveal fourteen girls whose religious affiliation is known. Three claimed to have no religion, three were Protestant and eight were documented as Roman Catholic.

Death ruled the Southwest for decades. Bisbee's water supplies were contaminated not only by outhouses, but by the city cemetery. Typhoid was rampant, malaria, alcoholism and mine accidents all hospitalized and killed a large percentage of the population. The Grim Reaper walked the streets stairs and hallways of the red-light district just as quickly as Main Street. In the harsh reality of early Bisbee, suicide was all too common among miners, gamblers and the ill-famed ladies. Although, Coroner's Inquests reveal these were often desperate cries for help. Too often the desired rescuer, a man that had enchanted one of the ill-famed temptresses never came. Carrie Bush, Bridget Gallagher, Rita Reese, Ethel Paterson and Clara Dodge ended their lives in the district. Each of these girls drank carbolic acid (phenol alcohol). This was commonly used as a disinfectant or took corrosive sublimate tablets (mercury dichloride) a treatment for syphilis. These girls suffered terribly from the effects of these corrosive chemicals before dying in agony.

Not all the red-light deaths were tragic suicides, Helen Tichnor, fell off a porch in a drunken state on the fourth of July 1909. She died from a fractured skull the next day. Grace Calipon succumbed to alcoholism.

The graves that could be located are all unmarked in sections of rocky desert soil with patches of dried brown grass, but they are all in the consecrated ground of the Old Catholic section of Evergreen Cemetery. Also, with at least Rita Reese, a Catholic mass is known to have been said at the funeral. These graves are not isolated by themselves, but rather intermingled among graves of Bisbee's more respectable citizens, such as members of Kinsella and Critchley families. The graves of Clara Dodge and Ethel Paterson are recorded to be in the Evergreen Cemetery, but could not be positively located. Irene Logan and Grace Calipon are probably buried in Evergreen Cemetery, but records of their grave's locations have faded with time. Hazel Dee is buried next to her husband in Evergreen Cemetery. She died in 1969 in her 70's.

Yet, with all their charms the girls of the ill-famed life still were considered second best. It was their *"chaste"* sisters that were preferred by most men. Instead of wild times, they offered the attraction of family, stability and a chance of someone to grow old beside.

A French postcard of an ill-famed lady. c-1910

# Denizens of the Underworld

Around 1884, the petite and dark-haired Irish Mag arrived in Bisbee. Although, she was probably not the first scarlet lady to come to Bisbee, she is the earliest that history has chosen to record. When she came to the community, there could have been hardly a more desolate and uncivilized place in the continental United States. Renegade Apaches roamed the hillsides hunting and raiding. The community was built of tents and simple wooden structures nestled in the canyon bottom. Crude smelters billowed sulfur rich smoke and the largest structure in town was the hoisting works of the Czar Mine. Here, Irish Mag found a small home on the west end of town with a green roof and next to the home of saloon keeper/ Sheriff Billy Daniels. Outside her residence she kept a green parrot in an oak tree. Passing miners instructed the bird with a *"colorful"* vocabulary. She gained a reputation for compassion when she cared for the body of Sheriff Billy Daniels after he was ambushed and killed by Apaches, a few miles outside of Bisbee. This soiled dove of the high desert permeated the town with her feminine charms. Her allure was strong enough, a prospector named a promising mining claim after her. It is possible that she helped finance the prospect, although there is no documentation. Legends state that she became wealthy from this claim, but this is unlikely. Records do indicate at least three other women did profit from sales of the property. It was not until 1901, the Irish Mag Mine struck its first ore 850 ft. below the surface. Irish Mag herself had long disappeared from Bisbee, by this time. Yet, the Irish Mag Mine blossomed like a cactus flower, filling the community with wealth and immortalizing the fallen woman, Irish Mag.

The Irish Mag Mine, c-1910

After, Irish Mag, the ill-famed ladies become temporarily hidden in the shadows of time. Clara Allen started House No. 41 on Naco Road sometime before 1892. This woman came to Bisbee as a wild young lady and stayed to at least 1902, before moving to Globe, Arizona. She is believed to be the longest working madam in the town. During this time, she evolved into a motherly figure who gave maternal and moral advice to the men and women of Bisbee. The lack of information about her house implies was generally quiet.

On May, 7th 1892, the law forming the red-light district in Bisbee came into effect and Clara Allen and the other ladies moved their businesses into Upper Brewery Gulch. The people of Bisbee looked at a red-light district as an unpleasant necessity. It was unrealistic that prostitution could be eliminated in the remote town dominated by single men. Yet, it was desired that the ladies be isolated from residential and business areas. Ill-famed houses were often rowdy and sometimes violent places. At least inside of the city limits the district could be somewhat controlled.

Mother Earth's treasures poured wealth into the community. Citizens began to accept Bisbee was not a boom town like, Tombstone and the mines were going to prosper long. In 1896, the Weekly Orb newspaper printed its first issue and began to record daily activities that were considered too minor to print in the nearby Tombstone Epitaph.

On May, 11 1899, the worn pebbles of the gulch trickled with blood. That Saturday night, Irene Logan a madam of the red-light district entered the saloon of Dora Garnett (Dora McCrellis/ McCillis), another red-light madam. She came bringing with her another woman and a man. These ladies operated ill-famed houses located across from each other on Brewery Gulch. Soon after entering the saloon the intoxicated women engaged in *"sarcastic remarks leading to cutting abuse"*, which was followed by flying lead from a six-shooter. Dora had told Irene and her female companion to leave several times. They initially refused, but finally the one woman left and Irene remained. The abuse continued and Dora pulled a six-shooter from behind the bar and fired twice. One bullet struck Irene in the neck and exited through her back, but the other missed. Irene died shortly after being wounded. The coroner's jury decided that Ms. Logan had died of murderous intent and Ms. Garnett was held with $15,000 bail. Soon after being jailed Dora had a breakdown and was transferred to the county hospital where she could walk around freely. The Oasis, a newspaper printed at Arizola, Arizona published, a sarcastic comment about the upcoming trial. "Some *of the most respectable young gentlemen in Bisbee (choir singers, Sabbath school teachers, etc.,) have been subpoenaed to attend the district court at Tombstone next Monday, to testify to the good moral character of Dora Garnett, who will be tried for her life, for killing a fellow cyprian at Bisbee some weeks ago."* Little is known about the proceedings of the trial, but by April 1901, she had returned and was working at Rose Miller's Place.

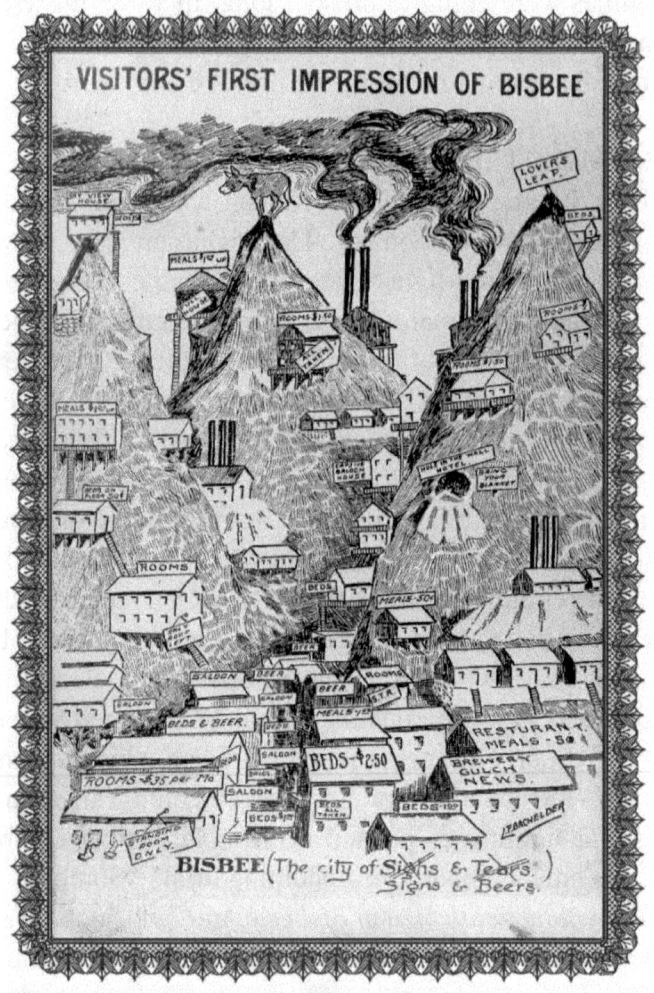

A humorous postcard poking fun at the living conditions in Bisbee, c-1903

As the turn of the century approached, Bisbee was conquered by the petite dark-haired Mexican beauty known as Anita Romero. She was described as a *"wild little animal"* with an unrestrained splendor. Joe Chisholm remembered, *"Her blue-black hair and shadowed eyes that were flaming glories of dull rose or lances of higher light with her moods, her luminous olive-cream skin that glowed pink or carmine with her flow of wild emotions, the all-around savage charm of her suggesting some strange barbaric strain,"*

Before Bisbee, she had traveled from Zacatecas, Mexico through the famed mining camps of Chihuahua, Cananea and Minas Prietas, but as with most of her profession she was a wanderer, staying only a short time at any given place. Anita began operating an ill-famed house and saloon as turbulent as her personality in late 1899. She first became entangled with the law in January 10, 1900, when she fought with another red-light girl, Juana Barba. Both ladies were intoxicated and they were fined and released.

First blood was spilled at Anita's place on April 29, 1900. Juan Valdez entered her saloon and Guillermo Fredrico was tending the bar. Valdez spent $9.00 on drinks and then asked to be given a room. Fredrico helped him to a bed. Then around 4 or 5 o'clock the girls of the house complained to Anita about him and she went to check on him. He was vomiting and asked her to bring him two drinks. She told him to see the bartender. He told her *"You whores have beat me out of this money, or beat me out of some money."* Anita told him that her girls were honest and never robbed anyone. Then, Anita questioned him if he had money, why did he ask for $1.75. Valdez told her, *"You pay me or this man Guillermo will pay me."* She responded that she would talk about it after he was sober. The discussion continued and became verbally abusive and he finally left. At 8:30, Anita's place was filled with music and crowded with people and Juan Valdez returned. He stepped up to the bar and said, *"Here you pimp (palo blanco)"* *"Neither you nor your whores are going to rob me out of a cent."* Anita was standing by the stove and said *"The bartender has nothing to do with the whores; I am the one who attended to them, and if you have anything against them you should talk to me about it"* Valdez left the bar and closed the door. As he left, he told Anita, *"You will see if you have any money or not."* He stepped back into the saloon and tried to shoot Anita. She was standing behind the bar. After the shot, Anita hid behind a demijohn. The other witnesses stated that Valdez tried to pull out a pistol, Fredrico shot first and Valdez's shot went through the roof. Firing continued back and forth. Anita stated, it seemed like she heard thousands of shots. The Americans in the house broke a window and went to get help, but one was shot in the hand. Estafina one of the girls was wounded. A man named Hulio (Julio?) took a bullet in the leg. Valdez reentered the saloon and moved towards the bar and was finally shot by Fredrico when he was about 4 feet from the bar. Valdez fell and began randomly shooting until he died. Pedro M. Garcia claimed that Anita fired twice at Valdez after he was down.

On December 18, 1900, Rosario Tapeta a man with a crippled hand was singing and Pedro Ariola was following along with a guitar outside of Anita Romero's Place. Then men went into the bar and had a drink and began quarreling in Spanish about a woman. Anita told them both if they wanted to fight to go outside. Pedro left and Rosario left about five minutes later. On the gulch the men met and began arguing again. Pedro pulled out a black-handled revolver and shot at Rosario. Rosario turned and tried to go back into the saloon. Two more shots were fired and Rosario fell. One bullet hit his collar bone, but was a minor wound. The other passed through his lungs and liver and proved to be fatal. Her house's reputation failed to improve.

The local newspaper responded by reporting that her bawdy house and saloon was frequented by a rough group of Mexican railroad men. Furthermore, it recommended it be shut down and claimed that the house cost the taxpayers hundreds of dollars a year in court fees. This was far more than her license fees. Less than a month later, violence again broke out at Anita Romero's place. Anita Romero heard that four men were headed up to her house and *"clean it out."* She told Deputy Constable Francisco Jurado, who was at the ill-famed house, about the predicted trouble. This deputy had been stationed to watch over the ill-famed houses and prevent trouble. He called Constable M. Doyle for assistance. Abundio Salas and Reyes Bustamante were there and had become *"insulting and abusive"*. Jurado searched the men and found no weapons. Constable Doyle and Deputy Constable John M. Johnson arrived and found no immediate problems and told Jurado to keep order and arrest anyone making trouble. Doyle and Johnson left. As they passed the Shattuck lumberyard, they heard four shots coming from Anita Romero's. They arrested a man running down the gulch and then found Jurado standing over the body of Abundio Salas, which was lying in the road. After Doyle and Johnson had left, Abundio and Reyes became abusive to the bartender and customers. Deputy Jurado, suggested to the men that they should go home. The men then began to shower the deputy with profanity. Jurado removed the men by force and arrested them. As Jurado was walking behind the arrested men in the darkness down the gulch, suddenly, Reyes punched Jurado and Abundio pulled out a .38 pistol and fired twice at the deputy. Jurado fired his .44 pistol once striking Abundio in the chest. As he fell, Abundio, fired a final shot and died quickly. Reyes Bustamante was arrested and fined $10.00, but did not have the money and spent the time in jail.

On March 1, 1901, Constable Johnson went up to Romero's to remove a drunken man, when he was jumped by the ladies of the house. Defeated he retrieved a gun and Constable Foster. The men arrested the women, but other than this the ill-famed house was quiet. Soon after this Anita Romero, the woman whose beauty made a man's blood boil, left Bisbee for the booming community of Cananea, Mexico.

A contemporary to Anita Romero was Mary Geary. This woman of African-American descent opened a house in Bisbee around 1897. Like Anita she operated a saloon connected to an ill-famed house. Other African American women worked at her establishment, like Emma Prather and Emma Hudson. A Miss Beach also worked for her, but her ethnicity is unknown. Regardless, her establishment served everyone and was frequented by *"Americans"* and Hispanics. On March 21, 1901, violence erupted at her house.

Sometimes there is thin strip of lace and a trickle of whiskey, between a law keeper and a law breaker. Deputy Constable and Deputy Sheriff John M. Johnson were headed up the gulch with John

Foster. They were warned than Francisco Jurado, a former deputy was at Mary Geary's place and had struck a man with a gun. He was acting wild and was likely to kill someone. Deputy Constables John M Johnson and John Foster were on their way up the gulch and Emma Hudson, a lady from Geary's house told Foster that Jurado was at Geary's house and *"raising hell."* Foster and Johnson walked to the house and could see Jurado sitting at the bar. The lawmen saw him get up and tell one of the girls that no one could ever arrest him. Jurado then left with three other men and headed towards Anita Romero's. The deputies decided to wait to arrest Jurado, because of the likelihood of an innocent bystander would be killed or injured. Johnson continued up to Rose Miller's Place, while Foster walked through Mrs. Geary's Place. One of the girls told Foster, she was afraid Jurado was going to kill her. He told her to get him if Jurado came back, then Foster went to Rose Miller's place to get a drink. As Johnson and Foster were being served their drinks, Emma Hudson came and told them *"For God's sake come over, come on as this man that is there is going to kill someone"*. She also warned them to allow Deputy Foster to enter first as Jurado was likely to kill Deputy Johnson on sight. Johnson went into the parlor and picked up his shotgun and both deputies headed to Geary's. They found Jurado leaning on the bar with his arms and told him to hand over his gun. There was a small scuffle. Johnson pulled Jurado down and Foster took his gun and put it in his pocket. As they were walking Jurado, asked Foster to loosen his grip on his arm. As soon as Foster loosened his grip, Jurado grabbed his gun from Foster. Foster shouted to watch out. Jurado turned and cocked the pistol and Johnson fired killing Jurado. By 1902, Mary Geary appears to have left Bisbee.

In December of 1901, Cora Miles purchased a property in Bisbee for $500.00 from John Reilly. This was likely "Pa" Reilly of the couple "Ma" and "Pa" Reilly who operated an ill-famed house on the gulch. "Ma" had been adopted as a child by a family who ran an ill-famed house and even though she was raised in that environment, she remained an unprofane, sober woman and true to her husband. She considered ill-famed houses her *"natural range"* of existence and felt she was meant to run a house. They had had ill-famed houses at the nearby Ft. Huachuca and Gleason, Arizona before settling in Bisbee. They had a reputation for caring about the girls who worked for them, feeling that they had only become lost along life's trails and were not truly bad people. They brought respectability and a *"Practical Christianity"* to the brothels.

Unlike, the Reilly's Cora Miles stood her ground firmly and was not hampered by morality. Although, her ill-famed house never was as lethal as Anita Romero's it was far from peaceful. A good part of the violence stemmed from Cora herself.

At 4:30 am on May 23, a typical red-light brawl broke out at Cora's house between Sydney and Grace Chase with Lillie Evans. Grace struck Lillie's head with a water pitcher. Leaving her covered in blood. Evidence must have indicated the guilt of both Grace and Lillie. They were both fined $5.00 each.

> **Wanted.—Man** to make himself useful around house. $1 a day and board. Apply after noon to Cora Miles, 48 Brewery gulch.  6-17 tf

Classified Ad, Bisbee Daily Review June 17, 1902 page 5

A few months later, Cora had Dolly Dunbar (Monbar) and May Hines arrested for throwing rocks at her establishment. A number of girls were drinking wine around the house at the time and it could not be confirmed that Dolly had thrown any rocks. Dolly, testified she was holding a bottle of Mumm's Extra Dry (champagne) and could not have thrown rocks. In true red-light fashion most of the witnesses failed to show up for court, so the city profited after Justice McDonald fined the absent witnesses $2.50 each for contempt.

August 3, 1903 a complex chain of events began. Cora attacked one of her girls, Phyllis Sherwood with an ice pick. Phyllis was wounded twice in the face, but Cora had a hand broken in the dispute. A few days later, Cora was arrested for assault with a deadly weapon. The case was later dismissed when it was revealed that Phyllis had attacked Cora with a beer bottle and Cora had only defended herself. At the same time Phyllis Sherwood and fellow soiled dove Sybil La Verne were arrested for allegedly stealing $575.00 in cash and bank certificates from customer, Bert F. Noftz on the night of August 4th. Cora Miles was the primary witness against the girls, but the evidence provided by Cora and the other witnesses was weak and the girls were released. As Noftz left the court room a man approached him and asked him if he was the man, who claimed the women had stolen money from him. He said, *"Yes."* and the man struck him a severe blow with his fist. The rumor went around town that Noftz had been stabbed, but this was untrue. Noftz continued to visit Cora's House and became involved with an ill-famed lady, Mabel Carlise who worked at the house. Noftz, Mabel Carlise and Johnny James met at the Wave Candy Parlor with a rented carriage. On August 19 at 12:50 am, Noftz and James entered the St. Louis Beer Hall with their faces covered with masks and guns drawn. They ordered the occupants to raise their hands, but the robbers were nervous and shot and wounded bartender Otto Schmidt. When roulette dealer L.O. Milless walked through a door he was shot and killed. Noftz and Ms. Carlise left Bisbee for Cananea, Mexico in the rented carriage. In Mexico, Ms. Carlise changed her name to Mabel Pearson. Bert Noftz, had been left in charge of the Opera Club House, while its manager was on vacation. During this time, Noftz had been spending club house money on Mabel Carlise in the red-light district. It was felt that Noftz had accused Phyllis Sherwood and Sybil La Verne stealing money from him to cover up his own theft of the Opera Club House funds. Noftz was sentenced to seven years in prison and was released after completing five years. Johnny James was not convicted for his part and Mabel Carlise was never tried.

The activities at Cora Mile's House were quiet only for a couple weeks. On September 3, 1903, a deputy sheriff was searching her house to locate a watch that was believed to have been stolen from one of her customers. Under a bed in an upstairs room, he discovered almost one pound of opium, a full layout with an opium pipe and needles. At the trial, most of the witnesses failed to provide significant evidence. This may have been due to the fact the majority of the witnesses were girls employed at the Mile's house. Pearl Philips had told officers that she had seen Cora and Joel Gibson smoking the pipe, but was struck with sudden amnesia during the trial. The case was dismissed and Cora's attorney insisted that the opium and pipe be returned to her.

The Cora Miles House mellowed for a time. At 2:00 am on November 29, 1903, a drunken Charley Coles proceeded to break all the glassware he could find and then continued to shatter the mirrors located behind the bar. The ladies of the house fled and the Coles stayed on the front porch until he was arrested.

By this time, Cora's success as a madam was in decline. In April of 1904, she was accused along with Goldie Allen of embezzlement. It is believed the case was settled out of court. By June 1904, the Cora Miles Saloon and red-light house was published in the classified ads for rent.

> **FOR RENT**—Cora Miles' saloon and residence, 48 Brewery Gulch. Furnished throughout. See Cora Miles, or address Box 237, Bisbee.

Advertisement, Bisbee Daily Review, June 5, 1904

Annie Levoie rented the property. Cora left town and married William Wortman. She adopted the name Cora Wortman. During October

1905, she was accused of robbing C. Willis of $700.00 in the red-light district at Phoenix, Arizona. She was arrested in Tucson, but months later the case was dismissed because the primary witness another red-light girl's testimony did not match the statements she had made earlier. Cora returned to Bisbee in 1906 and brought a suit against Annie Levioe for unpaid money. Cora and William did operate a business in the Upper Brewery Gulch as late as 1908. It is unclear of the nature of the establishment. It is possible it was a respectable commercial business. The couple were accused of defacing an American flag as they had attached words to the bottom for an advertisement. Both of the Wortman's were later cleared of these charges. Difficulties continued for Cora. William died on July 20, 1908 from consumption at nearby Benson, Arizona.

> **CARDS OF THANKS.**
>
> I desire to thank my friends for the many acts of kindness which they showed me during my bereavement following the death of my husband, William Wortman, and to assure them that they will ever be remembered with gratitude.
>
> (MRS.) CORA WORTMAN.

Notice in Bisbee Daily Review, July 24, 1908

After this, a number a lawsuits against Cora mounted. Each of these were for default of debt. Her property was sold in 1911 at a sheriff's sale for $2,700.00. The troublesome Cora Miles then disappears from Bisbee history.

In November of 1903, Bisbee was introduced to one of its least popular residents and operaters of #27 an ill-famed house, Con

(Cornelius) Shea. Shea and his wife Lillian Shea (Lillian Howard). They had come from Jerome, Arizona, where Con had been employed as a bartender. Soon after coming to Bisbee, he was arrested and fined $7.50 for assault and battery. The violence continued and at 11:30 pm on February 26, 1904, he became engaged in a disagreement with his wife in the red-light district. The resulting fight ended with Con kicking his wife in the head until she was reported to be unrecognizable. After being released on $300 bail he returned and assaulted her again. Con was re-arrested and released on $1000,00 bond. In the following days, the Bisbee Daily Review published a series of scathing articles about Con Shea.

*"This fiend in human form, is unfit to walk the same streets trod by little children. He is bereft of all decency and manhood and jails were built for the expressed purpose of keeping such as he."* The article ended with *"... This creature confined away frm the sight of honest men, in whose nostrils he has become a continual stench."*

March 1, 1904, the day of Con Shea's trial the Review published an article titled, *"Bisbee is on Trial."* In this firm article the Review make their opinion well known and advises the jury to, *"Do your duty gentlemen."* Con was convicted, even though his wife testified that the injuries were caused by a door. The Bisbee Daily Review published a thank you notice naming each individual juror. Shea was given sentence to pay a fine of $300 or 300 days in the county jail.

Lillian Shea was not the kind of woman to passively accept her situation. On December 15, 1904, she stabbed Con with a knife. The blade's deadly course was altered by a rib and saved Con's life.

New Years Eve 1905, an ill-famed girl known as Carrie Bush walked up to the bar next to Lillie Shea and ordered a lemonade and mumbled something about not living until 1906. When her lemonade arrived she swallowed a handful of corrosive sublimate tablets and washed them down with the lemonade. A doctor was called and her stomach was pumped. She lived for a time, but made it clear that if she survived, she would only try again. Con Shea tried to learn what her real name and where her family was, but she would only say, *" I am plain Carrie Bush and when I die, bury me in the Potters Field."* On January 9th, she succumbed. True to her wish she presently lies in a barren unmarked grave in Evergreen Cemetery.

Behind the low lying headstone is the barren plot of dirt that marks the location of Carrie Bush's grave.

The grave in the center of Rita Reese, outlined with a short cement wall

Funeral Record for Carrie Bush

    W.K. Lee sold his *"house"* in Lowell to Con Shea in November of 1905. It is believed the Shea's moved their ill-famed to outside of Lowell, Arizona at this time. The fledgling community was less than thrilled with the new *"business"* addition. Trouble soon followed. On November 23rd William Nichols assaulted Con and gave him a black eye. Two weeks later, the false rumor spread through Lowell that Con had been shot and killed. The Christmas Season continued to be exciting for the Shea's. Early in the morning on December 23, two men entered the house at 3:00 am wielding six-shooters and their faces covered with handkerchiefs and ordered everyone to put their hands up. They immediately walked up and took a gun that the Shea's kept hidden under a towel at the bar. This indicated that the men were familiar with the workings of the house. After securing $75.00 the men backed out of the house and made their getaway. Later, Charles White and William Rogers were arrested for the hold-up. The men were later released for lack of evidence.

In February 1906, Lillian's temper flared. Con had become too friendly with the house merchandise and Lillian smashed him on the head with a beer bottle and knocked him unconscious. She continued to beat him in his comatose state. A reporter from the Bisbee Daily Review called the house many times trying to get information about the fight. Each time a different girl answered the phone and stated she was busy and could not answer questions. The Shea house had developed a reputation as tough house and a petition had been raised to have its license revoked.

An American postcard of a girl on a candlestick telephone c-1910

The Shea's appear to have quieted down, until May of 1912, when Lillian had Con arrested for insanity because he was attempting to hurt his family. The charge was later dismissed. After this, the Shea's fade from Bisbee history. Cornelius Shea is believed to have died in Jerome, Arizona in 1913. How Lillian spent the remainder of her life is unknown.

In September 1907, J.H. Brown and Mrs. Annie Hooper were arrested in Lowell. Mrs. Hooper was charged with running a disorderly house and Mr. Brown was charged with vagrancy for living in a red-light house. They were held in the two-story jail in Bisbee. Upon release, Mrs. Hooper returned to the cold concrete and steel of the jail with a judge. This time she wanted to marry Mr. Brown. The constables seem to have little issue with the wedding and were willing to allow Mr. Brown out of his cell. A small crisis occurred when no one was willing to step up and give away the bride. "Frijoles" a local drunk and petty criminal with a reputation of spending more time in jail than out, rescued Mrs. Hooper. He gave the ill-famed bride away to the awaiting groom. After the ceremony Brown was locked up in his cell. Interestingly, Mrs. Hooper was 12 years, Mr. Brown's senior. J.H. Brown was 23 years-old on his wedding day.

Jake Kerner, operator of an ill-famed house known as No. 128 entered another red-light house. The establishment was known as the Canadian Club in Brewery Gulch and he wanted to play dice. It was September 19, 1908. At a nearby table Glen Langford was sitting down to play a game of poker. It was between 3 and 4 am. Former Constable and part owner of the Beer Garden in Lowell, Henry Hall entered the club. Hall was there to pay Harry Miller $25. Langford asked Hall to play poker and Hall declined. Offended, Langford wanted to know the reason why and Hall told him, *"If you want to know so bad, Langford. I will tell you. You have the reputation of being a cheater and I don't care to play."* Enraged at being called a cheater, Langford began a tirade of accusations and cursing towards Hall. During this entire time, Langford had a hand in his right pocket, grasping a .41 caliber double-barreled derringer. Finally, Langford said, *"Anybody who says I am a cheater is a god-damn-son-of-a-bitch-liar"* Langford put a foot on the seat of the chair he had been sitting on and said, *"let her go as she looks, if you want to go on through with it, go on."* Hall drew his gun and fired hitting Langford who turned. Then Hall fired a second shot. Mortally, wounded Langford fell to the floor of the saloon holding the derringer. As his body was rolled over to treat his wounds, the gun fell from his grasp and George Ball picked up the pistol. Ball handed the gun to Ollie LePaige, the Canadian Club's piano player. Ollie placed the derringer behind the bar. When Constable Twomey asked for the gun later, LePaige initially denied there had been a gun. After about a half hour discussion the constable convinced LePaige the seriousness of hiding the weapon. Glen Langford died at the Copper Queen Hospital on September 20$^{th}$, 1908. The inquest determined that Hall killed Langford in self-defense.

On September 7, 1909, the district livened up with fight between Lena Frush and Millie Brown. Jake Kerner and Jake Miller were nearby and when Millie began to get the best of the battle and gave Lena a firm blow to the lip. Kerner a companion of Ms. Frush, foolishly tried to intervene. After breaking up the initial fight, the brawl brewed up again and this time Millie was scratched around the face, struck on the head and kicked by Jake Kerner, *"where the sun don't shine."* In truth, all were losers and each paid fines. Kerner paid $30, Millie $25 and Lena paid $15. The Bisbee Daily Review reported, *"The trials were made the occasion for a parade of the painted denizens of the underworld and two or three of a choloate (sic) shade, most of them together with a number of male hangers-on, being requires as witnesses. There was a dozen or more witnesses in each case, and to the casual-spectator the courtroom and clerk's office, where the witnesses were herded, presented the appearance of a tenderloin convention headquarters."*

In less than a month, Lena found herself in *"wild and wooley hair-pulling match"* with Helen Blanchard. Helen owed Lena one dollar and on October 26, 1909 Lena asked for the money. This angered Helen and she stewed in anger until 2:00 am and she went to Lena's and broke down the door. She then proceeded to drag Lena out of bed, yank her hair and pound on her with rocks. This continued until Lena was *"unable to navigate"* For the trial the next day, Lena had to be transported to the court by a hack (passenger wagon). Ms. Blanchard plead guilty and was given a hefty $50 fine.

A silhouette of a red-light brawl by a French illustrator
c-1914

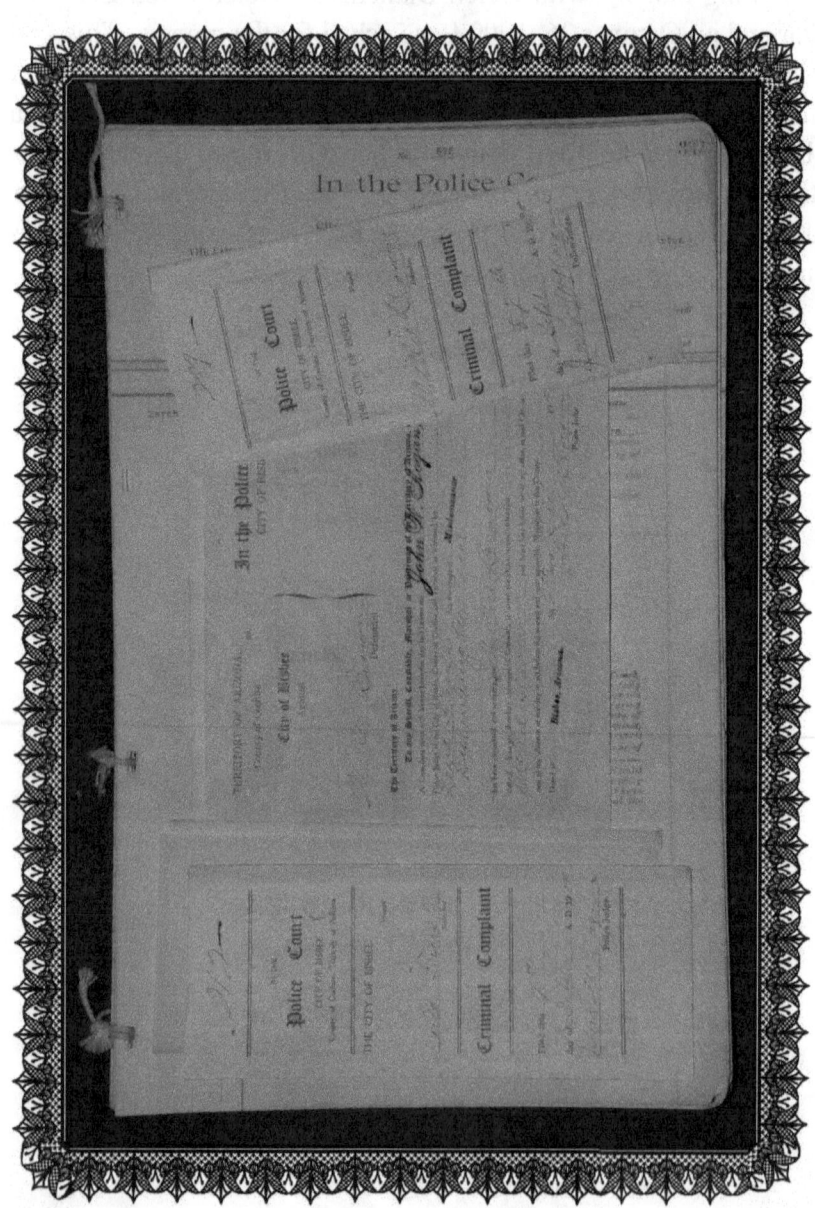

Justice Court records for the fight between Millie Brown and Lena Frush on September 7, 1909

Around 1903, Dollie Knapp began working in Bisbee's red-light district, under the name Dolly Monbar. Generally, it was the customers that discovered themselves with their valuables stolen in the red-light district. But on July 30, 1903, Dolly Monbar's ill-famed house was robbed and $350.00 was taken. Dolly was at a neighbor's resident and was clueless to who had committed the crime. Officer Casad did locate a suspect who had tried to pawn a lady's watch, but Miss Monbar stated it was not hers. Initially, money was often an issue with Dolly Monbar. At first this western Aphrodite gets into difficulties by not paying for cigars she purchased from the Las Dos Naciones Cigar Factory at Nogales, Arizona. The following year, A. LeRoy a dry goods merchant, sues her for $118. Dolly was taken to court and tried to get the judge to release her from the debt, because she was a single mother raising a son. Unfortunately, for Miss Monbar witnesses proved, the child actually belonged to her sister. She was held responsible for the debt. Her house appears to be relatively quiet. On August 10, 1905, she marries Thomas Alexander Dunbar and her name changes to Dolly Dunbar. The quiet times ended on August 8, 1906. Violence erupted in her house, No.41. This night, a drunken Ed Shearer asked Dolly if he could lie down and sleep on her couch in the bar room. Later, Jake Miller came in and pulled him off the couch. Dolly told him to leave the drunk man alone. Miller began using foul language and threaten to *"clean the house out."* Dolly's husband, Thomas went outside onto the porch steps to help in the situation. Jake threw a rock and struck Thomas on the jaw. He fell to the ground, unconscious with blood pouring from his mouth. Charles Madden began hitting Dolly and one of her girls, Fay Ellison smashed Charles with a chair. Marie Eddy was awoken by the disruption came onto the porch and was cut by a thrown rock. Thomas Dunbar suffered a broken jaw and a tooth broken in two. At the trial the defendants, Jake Miller and Walter Malen claimed they saw Thomas fall, but did not know why. Then they were suddenly attacked by four or five girls of the house wildly swinging chairs. As part of their story, they claimed Thomas was drunk, not realizing he abstained from alcohol and could not be inebriated. Attorney for the defense J.W. Ross closed with argument *"in which dwelled on the character of the women who were in the case and endeavored to discredit their testimony."* At the end of his argument, a man named Olsen who was watching the proceedings began supportively clapping. Olsen was taken to jail for this inappropriate outburst. Dolly's house remains subdued for a time. In June 4, 1911, trouble arises and an enraged Dolly tries to cut the throat of a customer, George Reardon with a straight razor. Luckily, she missed and only seriously sliced his leg. It required 17 stitches to seal the wound. The dispute was caused by Dolly's jealousy over Reardon's *"faithlessness"* Her case was initially submitted for Grand Jury, but in December 1911, it was rejected. Thomas Dunbar is granted a divorce for infidelity in July of 1911. On June 18, 1913, Thomas Dunbar died in Bisbee from heart failure. He was at 36 years old and is buried at Evergreen Cemetery. It is unclear what happened to Dolly. It is likely, she left Bisbee and was working in a house called No.12 at the red-light district at Tucson in 1912.

    A group of feisty hard–fighting girls appear in Bisbee's history around 1910. These were Dora Tyson, Hester Parker, Tempest Wyland and Marie Happe. During the night of May 5, 1911, a war broke out between two houses in the district and these ladies were active participants. It was settled when Dora Tyson and Marie Happe were placed under a $500 bond to keep the peace for six months.
After the battle the newspaper reported, *"Only the perfume of a dozen different attars remain in the court rooms as a reminder of the redlight war."*

    Hester had a reputation for trouble and was arrested every few months. First, Hester was arrested in 1909 for fighting with Marie Gusten. She was arrested again trying to remove her luggage from ill-famed house known as No.33 while there was a lien on her belongings. Dora Tyson made the complaint against her. March 29, 1911 was theoretically a wonderful day for Ms. Parker. The 22-year-old married Frank Haywood, a man 11 years her senior. Dolly, Dunbar and George Reardon were the witnesses to the marriage. Their happiness was short-lived. On June 4, 1911, she was fined $10.00 for fighting. Then nine days later, she learned her husband Frank

Hayward was going riding up to the Divide with another ill-famed lady, Mae Scott and a man named Davis. Hester rode a horse, recklessly through the city with a revolver hanging by her side. She caught up to the riders at the Divide and saw Mae lay her head on Frank's lap. Hester fired a shot at Haywood. The bullet missed and the gun was seized from her. All the bullets were taken out and the gun was tossed into the canyon below. After this Hester retreated back to town. According to the Bisbee Daily Review, when Officer Parley McRae arrested her, she told him *"She wanted to, "fill the ___ ___ ___ full of lead."* At the brief trial Hester stated that she asked Haywood to choose between herself and Mae. Her husband had chosen Mae. She was supporting a six-year-old son and because of this the attorney convinced the Judge Burdick Hester could not be convicted by a grand jury, she was acquitted. The following year she became entangled in a brawl with Fay Greer and was fined $7.50. After this she recedes from Bisbee history.

Mae Scott becomes embattled in a *"glass and head breaking affair."* with Molly Jenson in 1912. Although, it is settled with court fines, the Bisbee Daily Review suspected more trouble and describes it with a colorful euphemism;" *The two tribes of Apaches in the district are said to be at each other's throats and further outbreaks are feared".* Yet, the district generally, remained calm. That is until February 21, 1914.

The night of February 20th, Joe Oliver a bootlegger from Oklahoma, spent the night with Mae and left the house in the morning. Mae's husband, C.H. Smith a miner became concerned by Oliver and thought she needed to leave the ill-famed house. Smith began packing Mae's belongs. He was right, trouble was brewing. After leaving Mae, Oliver went to Uncle Sam's Pawn Shop and rented a pistol. When he returned Smith was still packing and Oliver called him outside. On the porch and under gun point, Smith was told to descend the steps. At this point Oliver shot Smith in the arm. According to the Bisbee Daily Review the bone was shattered and the arm was hanging only by the flesh. Joe ordered Smith to tell no one of the incident or he would come back and kill Smith.

Oliver was temporarily arrested by Officer Walter Brooks. Brooks noted, that Oliver was a cool character and mentioned to him about how much trouble he was in. Oliver responded *"Yes, it is a tough hole to get into, but there is always a way out."* The officers failed to carefully check his belongings. He had a hack saw! At 2:30 am, on February 22, the officers discovered a hole in cell door of the county jail. Three iron bars were cut off and four prisoners missing. Three men with short sentences remained in the jail. It is believed that the saw was in a purse that belonged to Oliver that contained five dollars and personal papers. Oliver had requested from Judge High that he be given them. Two of the escaped prisoners were jailed drunks and were quickly captured at Naco trying to cross into Mexico inebriated. Joe Oliver and J. Hamilton Evans were never apprehended. Although, it is not believed they went into Mexico. Oliver was described as *"a man about six feet in height, his face very wrinkled, and carrying a worried look. He wore a large hat and a gray shirt."*

May Gillis first appeared in Bisbee history in 1905, when she attempted to commit suicide at the Elite Lodging House. As was common at the time, she drank carbolic acid. Her subsequent screams of pain drew attention and her life was saved. In 1912, attention was again drawn to her when, she was arrested for operating a house of ill-fame on Broadway. Broadway is a narrow pathway between buildings that was used by school children to climb up from Brewery Gulch to Central School. The house of ill-fame was only 150 ft. from the school.

Looking up Broadway from Brewery Gulch.
The large building in the distance is the back of Central School.

May received a 60-day jail sentence and Victor Ritner the man arrested with her, had his case dismissed. Ritner was a miner for the Calumet & Arizona Mining Company and except for being injured a few times in the underground mines never was mentioned in the newspapers. That changed after he began spending time with May Gillis. Briefly, they tried to charge Ritner with *"white slavery"* then it was changed to adultery, but the case was dismissed. May was released from jail and she chose to use her time poorly. In August 1912, she tried to shoot Ritner with a revolver near the Sacramento Shaft in Upper Lowell during an argument. Victor took the gun away from May. Both May and Victor were arrested. Ironically, Victor was charged with possession of a deadly weapon, even though it was the gun he had taken away from May. He avoided being a satisfactory

69

witness for the prosecution against May and she could not be charged with attempted murder. She received 90 days in jail and he received 15 days in jail and a hefty $75 fine.

May was in and out of jail for a time, then in August 1916 she was declared insane and sent to an asylum. By 1920, she had returned to Bisbee and continued her rocky relationship with Ritner. On July 19, 1920 a 39-year-old Mamie (May) Gillis finally married the 46-year-old Victor Ritner. The Ritner's resided in Bisbee for the remainder of their lives, passing away in the 1940's

With the Mexican Revolution and a number of casualties on the American side of the Border, American soldiers were stationed at Naco, Arizona. On March 5, 1916, one of district's African-American ladies, Irene Brown ran into trouble with a soldier from the Tenth U.S. Cavalry. In the privacy of her quarters, he robbed her of two dollars by threatening her with a straight razor. Fortunately, he did not get far before he was arrested. A few months later, in September, the Bisbee Daily Review reported a National Guard Unit of Native Americans had returned from a ten-day hike and a pay day. *"For a time it appeared as though the Indians' and others would sack, burn and bury the property in the Gulch."* They did quiet down and the Provost Guard came up from Naco and cleared out any late stragglers. Soldier, John P. Hayes made a poor choice when he robbed an unnamed soiled dove of two watches, a pocketbook and $14.00. He was arrested and turn over to the Army for discipline.

Florence Sharp was one of the last legal madams of Brewery Gulch. Ornery and determined, she first ran into trouble in February 1917 when she was caught violating prohibition by having whiskey. She continued to tangle with law enforcement. In late March-April, Florence was arrested for disturbing the peace. After her arrest and fine, she harassed police officers in the district. The officers finally, arrested her for vagrancy and she was fined $75. Her first arrest for violating Prohibition had little affect and she was charged for alcohol possessions in June 1917. The last mention of her is in early July 1917 when she was fine $25 for using obscene language.

As the district closed in early December 1917, the women dispersed quickly. Only, two of the ladies from the period of the legal prostitution are recorded to have remained in town. One, who is only known as Hazel Dee became Mrs. Emmett Walsh and lived in Bisbee, until she died in 1969. May Gillis eventually became Mrs. Victor Ritner. In 1940, the Ritner's were living at 205 Van Dyke Street in Warren. At the time, Victor was 65 years-old and Mary was 60. After a lengthy hospital stay, Victor Ritner died on November 25, 1941 and Mary continued to live in Bisbee, but died on May 22, 1943 at the Cochise County Hospital in Douglas, Arizona.

An intimate French postcard. c-1907

# Dens of Dreams

A charming girl budding from poppy blossoms

eeply imbedded in history has been the intimate link between pleasures provided by the female and those provided by substances. Chemical seductresses were also available in the depths of the red-light. Although, opiates were widely available in Bisbee. Generally, these were patent medicines that contained opium and could be purchased at drug stores. These were medical proprietary concoctions of chemicals and often contained significant amounts of alcohol, cocaine and/or opiates. They claimed to cure any variety of human afflictions. In those pre-antibiotic times when diseases were poorly understood, the sick often turned to these for help. They were readily available at drug stores throughout Bisbee. Unfortunately, these patent medicines could be highly addictive and dangerous. Yet, patent medicines did not acquire the strong negative reputation, like smoking opium

**N**O **MORE "DOPE."**
The announcement comes from Central Pharmacy, the popular drug store, on Brewery avenue, that no more cocaine, opium or morphine will be sold by them after January 1st. This will be a hard blow to "dopers," but is certainly a moral to be followed by all stores selling the "stuff."

Announcement from Bisbee Daily Review December 16, 1909

Opium is derived from *Papaver somniferum,* better known as the opium poppy. The flower has been grown for centuries to serve ornamental and medicinal needs. Opium poppies produce a white, latex, sap with a disagreeable taste. This sap deters herbivores from eating the plant. Farmers collected the sap by carefully cutting into the plant's unripen seed pods. The liquid latex was allowed to slowly ooze out and then was scraped off. After, the sap dried it was processed to become smoking opium or in some cases one of medicinal opioids.

The Central Pharmacy and the Justice Court c-1908

In 1909, the police predicted that at least three locations in the red-light district had *"smoking"* opium available. The opium den offered a different experience and was not as simple as drinking from a medicine bottle. Substantial equipment was needed, for opium is not truly smoked, but rather vaporized. The smoker needed to prepare raw opium by *"cooking."* Also, opium *"smokers"* contrary to modern beliefs preferred company and desired a social environment, not solitude. The distinct lack of a Chinese population in Bisbee allowed the scarlet ladies of the red-light district to fill this niche in the economy of vices.

According to H.H. Kane a late 19$^{th}$ century opium expert, the long pipes were made with a bamboo stem. As the pipe was smoked the yellow bamboo turned a lusterous black and became permeated with opium giving the smoke/vapors and unusual flavor. Bowls were made of hardened clay. The bowls and stems were sometimes instead, made of stacked rings of lemon peel glued together then carved and polished. The lemon provided a pleasant scent to the smoke. Expensive pipes were works of art with silver and ivory decorative fittings.

Components of an opium layout:

*Lamp that burns peanut oil
or sweet oil
Scissors
Opium box
Tray
A curved bowl cleaner
Straight bowl cleaner
Needle for cooking opium
Tray for hold opium ashes
Sponge for cleaning the bowl*

An opium layout

To begin the smoker lit the lamp and *"cooked"* the opium. They placed a syrupy mass of opium upon the needle and heated it carefully above the burning lamp. Slowly , the color changed from a dark to a golden yellow streaked with black as the opium swelled to six times its original size. The drug was rolled along the bowl and drawn out into thin strings to *"cook"* the substance throughally. After a cooked pea-sized pellet of opium was formed, it was placed into a hole in the bowl of the pipe . The bowl was placed over the lamp, slowly heating the opium. Then the needle was used to pierce the pellet. Then the opium was ready to smoke. A smoker leaned over the lamp and heated the opium until it began to vaporize. The smoker either breathed in the vapors with either one long draw or several short draws, exhaling through the nose. This process was completed four or five times for a beginner or 100 time an experienced smoker. Opium ashes were saved and ingested or sold to poorer smokers Legend told that women should not smoke an expensive pipe. The moisture from their lips was supposed to cause the pipe to split.

The opium vapors produced nausea, itchness, dizziness then a *"dreamy state of wakefullness"* Sexual desire was increased with a sense of calming peace and contentment. Experienced opium users would introduce young girls to opium with the main intent of seducing them after the opium increased their sexual desires. It was noted that women risquely loosened their corsets and removed their shoes in the company of strangers while in opium dens. During the 1880's, in San Franciso three ill-famed ladies were challenged to see who could smoke the most opium for a $50.00 prize The three girls smoked nearly half a pound in 30 hours.

French trading card c-1905

Regardless, opium is a harshly addictive goddess of pleasure and those who seek to cease their relationship with her are doomed to an extended period of torment.

A French anthropormorphic postcard depicting humans as insects and an opium poppy as a woman. She is sprinkling poppy seeds. c-1903

A postcard series #532 with a French girl and a full Opium layout and pipe. c-1910

A French girl choosing an opium needle c-1910

A French girl placing opium in the bowl of an opium pipe. c-1910

Heating the opium over a lamp. c-1910

81

Piercing the opium pellet with a needle. c-1910

Another view of a French girl with a full Opium layout and pipe. c-1910

A rarer postcard of a French girl with opium layout. c-1910

Another difficult to find postcard of a French girl with a full Opium layout and pipe. c-1910

A rarer postcard of a French girl with a full Opium layout and pipe. c-1910

The first recorded arrest for opium use in Bisbee was in 1902 when Charles Ritz was arrested with his complete layout and pipe. The Bisbee Daily Review stated, *"In fact the fumes of the dried poppy penetrated the thick sulphur atmosphere and came floating down the gulch toward the police court... He was dreaming guilty in his cell last night, but couldn't see a hundred dollars to bail him out."*

The Copper Queen Smelter c-1902

The sulphur fumes is a reference to the smoke from the Copper Queen Smelter which permeated the early community. His arrest was followed the next year by the arrest of red-light madam, Cora Miles and Joel Gibson. Naco, Sonora was thought to be source of opium and this was at least partially true. In 1906, eighteen people including several Bisbee residents and a woman were arrested after being discovered smoking opium in Naco, Sonora. Even women were

Suspected of smuggling opium from Naco into Bisbee. After C.E. Biddenger and B.A. Lacey were arrested for possession of cocaine and pipe opium, they claimed to have purchased the drugs in Warren. The police interrogated an important Warren resident who responded. *"Sure Mike," "Why I'm one of the stockholders. What are you going to do about it?"* The source of the opium was never positively determined to be from Warren, although the police searched the area intensely. The two men told the arresting officers, how they learned to smoke opium in the Chinatown at San Francisco.

During 1908, a letter published in the Bisbee Daily Review brought opium dens temporarily to the forefront of concern.

*"Bisbee, Ariz, June 2, 1908*

*Mr. John Stevens,*

*City Marshall"*

*"I will try to see if you will enforce this letter. It is in regard to a negro opium joint which my son frequents day and night with women of the red-light district. I have went after him several times and he always comes home sick and broke and unless it is broke up soon we can't have money to buy bread. He says he spends his wages and can't keep from it, so you do me and my little girl a favor by breaking it up at once. The location is up Brewery Gulch on the left hand side in the back of the colored prostitute house in a building that's an old hack stand. Under there is several negro men and three or four white girls every morning between 3 and 4 o'clock.*

*"A Mother"*

The den was raided, but since smoking opium was not illegal, the men including Walter Dean and Merrill Gilland were charged only with vagrancy. During the arrests an unusually beautiful and well used opium pipe was seized. The stem was bamboo decorated with silver and ivory.

In the following years, a few arrests were made and layouts and pipes were seized along with any opium. In 1911, Pete Cook was arrested for having a *"Snow Party,"* (cocaine) but the police noted that the room was arranged like an opium den with mats on the floors and chairs against the walls. While investigating the theft of $600.00 worth of jewelry from ill-famed lady, Mamie Williams they located an opium layout in the possession of Abe Fields a man who followed carnivals. The layout included a beautiful pipe of fine workmanship and opium ashes.

A French girl with an opium pipe, c-1912

Opium arrest quieted down until 1916, when officers noticed two men and two women enter a building on Naco Road owned by *"Monte Jack"* a frequent guest of justice courts. Upon entering the property officers discovered opium, needles and a cooking lamp, but no pipes. Fannie Evans, Tom Evans, Will Martin and Edith Darnell were charged with smuggling opium. Tom Evans is believed to have owned the opium layout. He was later sentenced to one year in prison. Fannie his wife was released. The last noted arrest of smoking opium was in 1916, when police arrested Dollie St. Clair and George Warren at the Ozark House. Originally, the officers could not find a smoking layout, but during a second search they discovered the pipes, layout, lamps, opium ashes, opium, morphine and powder cocaine, *"Snow"*.

Opium dens did exist in Bisbee. At any given time there were a small number of dens in the red-light district, but in comparison to the number of arrests for drunken brawls the problems caused by smoking opium were small. Although, it may have been devastating to an individual or family, the community was faced with more serious issues, such as typhoid.

Sheet Music c-1908

# Women Enslaved

French postcard c-1908

Near the U.S. Mexican border, Bisbee's location made the white slavery issue more prominent than communities in the interior of the United States. In the late 19th and early 20th centuries, a *"White Slave"* was defined as a woman who has been brought into the immoral life of the red-light. Laws were passed to theoretically protect women from being forced into prostitution by the numerous proprietors and madams of ill-famed houses and those that procured women for them. The original purpose of these laws was built on good intention and then were corrupted with enforcement and liberal interpretations of the laws. Women of the red-light were pitied, but still given a level of dignity and respect. This was a sharp contrast to procurers and pimps who were held in vile and contempt. Where a prostitute could be considered a victim of social conditions. Procurers and pimps were committing a grave social crime by greedily profiting from the sins of others and at times against their will. The community found little mercy for these individuals.

There is little doubt women and girls were forced into the ill-famed life in Bisbee. Felix Taylor, was the only man prosecuted in the community for this action. The circumstances which may drive a woman to prostitution were common. Poverty dominated sections of the community, like Tintown and Zacatecas Canyon. Employment opportunities for an unmarried woman, widow or wife of a cripple was extremely limited. Bisbee was home to a significant number of young widows. Nationwide women of this nature were prey for men and women seeking to induce them into the red-light lifestyle. Over 200 men were killed in the mines alone, during the red-light district's years of operation. A larger number were crippled. This number does not include men killed at the smelters or the railroad. Both of these industries were also notoriously dangerous. Although, it was diseases that killed and crippled the majority of men. Youthful innocence, the allure of excitement and independence were other draws to the red-light life style. Arthur McKerrarcher, Mrs. Andy Miller and Mrs.

Kathryn Mabry found themselves at odds with law enforcement, by using these enticements to lure young girls.

Before 1910, when the "White Slave Traffic Act" also known as the Mann Act was passed, laws already stated that any immigrant woman who turned to the ill-famed lifestyle before she had lived in the United States three years could be deported. Arrests were made and women were deported.

This happened to Lily Silver, a French girl of extraordinary beauty. She had first entered the United States in 1908 along with two other French girls and two Frenchmen. Although, she was promised a high-paying position as a waitress, as soon as she arrived Lily began work as an ill-famed lady. She was arrested and deported back to France. Lily returned to the United States and speaking little English continued the ill-fame lifestyle. This time, she was arrested in Bisbee and was going to be deported again. Albert Telley, a young man from Bisbee offered to marry her to prevent the deportation. Lily Silver was not the only young woman who was promised high paying employment only to learn it involved working in a red-light district. In 1906, the Sherwood sisters were contracted in Chicago to come to Bisbee and work at the People's Theatre for $70.00 a week. When they arrived, the girls discovered that the theatre was located in the heart of Bisbee's red-light district. Fortunately, they sought the advice of a lawyer who explained they could not be forced to work in the district.

It was not until 1909 that *"white slavery"* was drawn to the forefront. Charles T. Connell was assigned as an immigration inspector for the Southwest. Mr. Connell spent time investigating ill-famed houses from El Paso thru New Mexico to Phoenix. Bisbee was part of his territory. He spent his investigations focused on international smuggling of girls. The inspector had a reason to be interested in Bisbee. August Contreras had been arrested for importing Mexican women to work at the Little Club in 1904. Frenchman, Emile Lefebvre proprietor of the Canadian Club and his *"wife"* Marguerite

Lefebvre quickly attracted Connell's interest. Connell sent a letter to the immigration inspector in San Francisco requesting information on the couple who were believed to have operated the Cozy Corner Saloon and a dance hall in Goldfield, Nevada.

Abraham A. Rosenwald was the next Bisbee resident that interested Connell. Unfortunately, Rosenwald was arrested in Bisbee on a vagrancy charge and Rosenwald, Sadie Kline and Ida Rosenwald left Bisbee, before Connell could gather enough information to charge Rosenwald with importing ill-famed women.

In 1910, after, Connell investigated Bisbee's red-light district, the Mann Act was passed. This legislation made it illegal to transport women across state or international borders for an *"immoral purpose."* The government was left to define immoral.

Problems developed with the *"white slavery"* law with cases like, the arrest of Mexican Revolutionary General Ignacio L. Pesquiera. He had been waiting in the United States, until he was ordered to return to Mexico to become Military Governer of Sonora for Carranza's army. The 65–year-old man had traveled with Senora Maria Rodriquez, a 23 year-old married woman. Even though their relationship was consensal, General Pesquiera was arrested. They were held on a white slavery charge at Douglas, Arizona for 10 hours until a $1000.00 bond was raised. This incident made it clear that the law was going to be used to arrest men traveling with women for an immoral purposes, even though the women were not prostitutes and any sexual relations were consensal and non-commercial.. Through a *Caminetti vs the United States* the U.S. Supreme Court upheld the law's use in this manner. The law was also interpreted to mean that it was illegal to pay for any transportation of ill-famed ladies. The Bisbee Daily Review stated the law was written, so vaguely that if a man gave a red-light girl a nickel to take the street car from Lowell to Bisbee, he had committed *"white slavery."* Pauline Wells was arrested in Douglas, Arizona in 1911, for paying for the railroad fare of two ill-famed ladies from Tucson to Bisbee. A few months later,

Harry Miller a resident of Bisbee was charged with white slavery after purchasing a railroad ticket for a lady from El Paso to Bisbee. He disappeared forfeiting a $2,500.00 bond. If the intent of the law was to prevent the importation of large numbers of immoral women then it failed. White slavery arrests continued to be made, but normally centered around individual girls not large numbers of women being imported. During 1913, Augustine Daley was arrested after he sent money to Lugarda Ensinas to travel from Nogales to Bisbee.

A street car heading from Lowell to Bisbee c-1910

In early 1914, the U.S. Federal Government wanted to capture Felisalio Simons. He was wanted for white slavery, kidnapping and suspected of murder. Simons had kidnapped three men in Baja, Mexico including his consort's Amelia Sanpey's father. A few feet from the U.S border Amelia's father was murdered. Unknowing that Simons had killed her father Amelia travel to Los Angeles and then to Bisbee. At Bisbee, she took up residence in the red-light district for one month. After which enticed by the lure of Mexican silver, she moved to Aqua Prieta, Sonora Mexico. In order to catch Simon, the law enforcement officers which included Bisbee City Marshall,

The dramatic cover of one of Clifford G. Roe's books on white slavery.
c-1911

French postcard c-1910

Bassett Watkins and Officer Walter Brooks, U.S. Marshall James McDonald and Secret Service agent Breinniman had a Mexican man offer Amelia money to come to a "*disreputable roadhouse*" in Pirtleville, Arizona. (near Douglas) The officers suspected that Simon would follow Amelia across the border to take the money from her. Knowing that the roadhouse would be filled with friends of Simon, the officers wanting to avoid bloodshed, the pulled up to a side door of the building. They entered the room and arrested Simon, Amelia and another man before anyone knew what was happening. Simon and Amelia were transported to Bisbee and the undescribed man was released. During the road trip to Bisbee, Simon made it clear he had not intended to be taken alive.

Each following years, a few arrests were made most of these small cases involving a man and a woman traveling together, but were not married. Miner, Joseph Griffith went to England and met a Cornishwoman, Susan Ferrell in 1915 and promised to marry her. She sailed from England to Ellis Island and was allowed entry to the U.S. due to her planned marriage with Griffith. The marriage was expected to occur on her arriving in Bisbee in November. By February 1916, they still not married and Ferrell filed a charge of white slavery against Griffith. A promise of marriage was often used to lure young women into a life of prostitution.

In 1922, an interesting case appeared. Two men were charged with white slavery for transporting two girls into Mexico for immoral purposes. Seventeen-year-old Opal Humpherys and 19-year-old Lillie Saathoff, both Bisbee girls went to Nogales, Sonora Mexico to work in the cabarets. The girls were immediately arrested when the crossed the Mexican border into Nogales, Arizona. William Stanton and Fred Davis, the men were arrested on this white slavery charge.

The white slavery issues appear to actually have been much smaller in reality than in fiction. Movies, books and vaudeville plays had inspired the public to see white slavery as a bigger problem than it actually was. The investigations of Immigration Inspector C.T. Connell reveal that in at least the in the Southwest the far majority of ill-famed ladies were American born. In 1916, the Bisbee Daily Review reported that the law had resulted in more harm than good. Since the law had been applied to all women, not only prostitutes a large number of black mail issues had arisen. The Review felt the law should be repealed and *"It has made the Federal Government a meddler in private affairs and a silent partner to blackmailers."*

Yet, the anti-white slavery movement, a crusade strongly pushed by Christian religious groups, developed enlightened solutions that were controversial for the time. These ideas blended well with the women's suffrage movement. Arguably, the most significant was the idea that women should be paid a fair wage that enabled them to adequately support themselves. A more radical suggestion was the idea that all children should be taught sex education. Children should be educated in heterogeneous groups and be taught age-appropriate lessons about sex in three formats, parental, religious and scientific. The subject would start with ten-year-olds and continued until the end of schooling. Reaching into biblical stories the anti-white slavery movement focused on references to the Prodigal Son and Mary Magdalene. The member of movement argued that a *"prodigal son"*, son who had left his early 20$^{th}$ century family to live a wayward and sin filled life could return home and be forgiven and accepted with open arms. Yet, a *"prodigal daughter"* was sneaked into the home, thru the backdoor and was forever tarnished. The movement sought to remove the double standard of morality based on gender and provide *"Christian forgiveness"* to ladies of the red-light. Conditions for women were moving forward.

French postcard c-1910

French postcard c-1912

# Bisbee's Captivatingly Wild Daughters

**Adams, Elsie:** This 19-year-old worked at the Canadian Club in 1909 and had lived in Bisbee one year. Originally, she was from Kentucky and her parents' names were Charles E. Cornell and Blanch Cross.
Copper Queen Hospital Patients Register July 30, 1909 Bisbee Mining and Historical Museum, Bisbee.

**Babcock, Bessie:** She worked in the tenderloin district in 1911 and was arrested for fighting and disturbing the peace.
"Decision in Brown and Banderman Cases" Bisbee Daily Review 25, July 1911 page 6

**Bacon, Mary Alice:** See Mrs. Fredrick Fuss.

**Banta, Maggie:** She was accused for living at a red-light house and not paying her room rent. Her case was presented by lawyers and the testimony given by other soiled doves did not end until 10:00 pm. A verdict of not guilty was presented at midnight.
"Woman is Acquitted of Beating Room Rent" Bisbee Daily Review 27, July 1907 page 5

**Beach, Miss:** She worked in the district in 1901 and likely at or near the Hog Ranch.
"Cochise County Coroner's Inquest #4" Arizona State Archives Phoenix

**Beaumont, Ada:** This lady was seriously if not mortally injured while riding a rented horse along Naco road. The newspaper reported that she was refined and had come from a fine family in Lexington, Kentucky. Her fellow ill-famed ladies help her pack her belongs to return home to likely die and removed anything that would indicate her illicit past to her mother. The Copper Queen Hospital records contradict at least partially the newspaper's story. It indicates she had lived in Bisbee for 14 of her 25 years and that her mother was deceased. Her father, Alfred B. Grubb was living in Spears, Kentucky. Mrs. J.G. Jones of 706E Main St. Lexington, Kentucky was her sister and she had an uncle, Will Holman of Athens Georgia. She was released from the hospital August 18, 1907 in improved condition. A year earlier, she accused Otto Henkel of stealing a saddle and bridle.

"In Police Circles" Bisbee Daily Review 14, August 1906 page 3
"Goes Home Dying and Broken Hearted" Bisbee Daily Review 28, August 1907 page 5
Copper Queen Hospital Patients Register July 27, 1907 Bisbee Mining and Historical Museum, Bisbee.

**Befil, Juana:** She was born in 1878 and immigrated into the United States in 1899. Juana worked with Anita Romero.

U.S. Census Bureau (1900). Bisbee, Arizona Territory, Cochise County District 0007,

**"Bertha":** Her fine clothes and jewelry were stolen in a burglary in the red-light district in 1904.

"Burglars Successful up Brewery Gulch" Bisbee Daily Review 13, April 1904 page8

**"Big Foot Lil":** This girl worked at the Shea House near Lowell in 1906.

"Cananea Visitor Lost His Money" Bisbee Daily Review 22, March 1906 page 4

**Bird, Virgil:** She attempted suicide by drinking *"Lysol"* solution after Oscar Johnson was arrested.

"Officer Kempton was Life Saver" Bisbee Daily Review 5, December 1912 page 6

**Black, Clara:** Originally, from Iowa, Clara worked with Dora Tyson. She was 24 in 1914.

U.S. Census Bureau (1910). Bisbee, Ward 1 Arizona Territory, Cochise County District 0005

**"Black Fanny":** She stabbed a baseball player named White with a stiletto dagger.
"Ball Player is Stabbed" Bisbee Daily Review 21, August 1902, page5

**Blanchard, Helen:** In 1909, she made the local news by getting into a fight with Lena Frush.
"Woman is Heavily Fined for Fight" Bisbee Daily Review 28, October 1909 page 8

**Bolan, Ray:** A feisty lady, she was arrested for fighting, but was so drunk the judge refused her bail, until she sobered up.
"Women in Fight" Bisbee Daily Review 16, January 1908 page 5

**Bond, Nellie:** This woman started an uproar when in 1905, she drunkenly walked through Lowell, completely nude.
"Woman Paraded Streets Naked" Bisbee Daily Review 29, June 1905 page 5

**Brown Bessie:** During 1914, she worked at the Mascot in Brewery Gulch. Although, she was born at Fort Riley, Kansas, the 19-year-old had lived in Arizona 16 years. Her mother lived at 720 Avenue G in Douglas Arizona. On June 15, 1914, she was hospitalized for two days for mercury dichloride poisoning.
Copper Queen Hospital Patients Register June 15, 1914 Bisbee Mining and Historical Museum, Bisbee.

**Brown, Helen:** She was fined $50.00 for discharging firearms in 1908.
"Fined $50" Bisbee Daily Review 20, May 1908 page 7
"Six Cases Arise From Two Originals" Bisbee Daily Review 22, May 1908 page 5

**Brown Irene:** One of African-American ladies of the gulch. In 1916, a soldier from the Tenth U.S. Cavalry tried to hold her up with a straight razor. She came from Texas and was 36-years-old in 1910.
"More Trouble Had" Bisbee Daily Review 7, March 1916 page 6
U.S. Census Bureau (1910). Bisbee, Ward 1 Arizona Territory, Cochise County District 0005,

**Brown, Millie:** During 1909, she engaged in a fight with Lena Frush.

103

"Bisbee Courts Grind out Grist" Bisbee Daily Review 8, September 1909 page 1
"Redlight Mixup is Finally Settled" Bisbee Daily Review 11, September 1909 page 1

**Burch, May:** Ms. Burch was brutally attacked by Verna Williams with a knife. She was cut three times across the face and required eleven stitches. It was considered a miracle she did not lose an eye.
"Assaulted her Companion with a Knife" Bisbee Daily Review 27, December 1908 page 8

**Burns, Carmen:** Accused of stealing $10.00.
"Charges Theft" Bisbee Daily Review 9, November 1907 page 7

**Burns, Nellie:** Attacked Belle Walker with a knife in 1908.
"Negress Wields Knife" Bisbee Daily Review 20, October 1908 page 7

**Bush, Carrie:** This lady worked at house No. 27 that was operated by Con Shea in 1905. She committed suicide by drinking carbolic acid. Although, her real name was not actually, Carrie Bush. This is the name her newspaper, funeral and burial records list her.
"Cochise County Coroner's Inquest #244" Arizona State Archives Phoenix

**Bustamante, Manuwello Miss:** This girl was arrested with Miss Jesus Curenza for violent intoxication, but the charges were dismissed.
"Warm Time in Tenderloin" Bisbee Daily Review 31, August 1904 page 1

**Calipon, Grace:** A known heavy drinker and resident of Bisbee of five to six years, suddenly she died on November 23, 1905. Grace worked at No. 41.
"Woman Drops Dead" Bisbee Daily Review 23, November 1905 page 5

**Carey, Minnie.** This was the mother of red-light madam Mabel Hastings. While residing at No.41, she overdosed on morphine and died. Although, her friends and family felt her death was accidental. Dr. C.L. Caven, the attending physician, believed the morphine tablets were taken with suicidal intent. Minnie died on January 18, 1903. She was 48-years-old and from Albuquerque, New Mexico.

"Cochise County Coroner's Inquest #114" Arizona State Archives Phoenix

**Carlise, Mabel:** In 1903, she was accused of aiding and abetting the murderers of L.O. Milless, Johnny James and Bert Noftz. She had traveled to Cananea, Mexico with Bert Noftz, one of the accused murders and his son. During her travels to Mexico, she went under the name, Mrs. Pearson. While waiting in the county jail she protested her incarceration, stating the Mexicans in jail sickened her with tobacco smoke and a Chinaman was in the cell next to hers. She also stated there was no place for her to sleep. These charges were later dismissed.

"Officers have in Custody Supposed to have Murders" Bisbee Daily Review 1, October 1903 page 4
"Noftz not yet Extradited, But Woman is in Bisbee" Bisbee Daily Review 3, October 1903 page 4
"Carlise Woman Consults Lawyer" Bisbee Daily Review 14, October 1903 page
"Cochise County Coroner's Inquest #870" Arizona State Archives Phoenix

**Casey, Aden:** In 1910, Aden was 25-years-old and from Missouri. She lived with Marie Gusten.

U.S. Census Bureau (1910). Bisbee Ward 1, Arizona Territory, Cochise County District 0005

**Casey, Helen:** Operated the Little Club in 1909.

Connell, C. T. (1909, April, 20). Untitled letter [Letter to Commissioner General of Immigration]. Office of Inspector in Charge, Douglas, Arizona.

**Casey, Myrtle:** She was in a fight with Mary Eddy in 1910. (Marie Eddie?) Charles Lannon was later arrested for giving her cocaine.

"Court Day Given to Undesirables" Bisbee Daily Review 25 June 1910 page 5
"Cocaine Dealer Fined" Bisbee Daily Review 10 November 1910 page 5

***"Catalina":*** Worked at Anita Romero's Place in 1900.

"Cochise County Coroner's Inquest #437" Arizona State Archives Phoenix

**Chase, Grace:** This girl worked in the Cora Miles house in 1902. She was arrested with Sydney Chase for striking Lillie Evans with a water pitcher and fined $5.00.

"Cut with Water Pitcher" Bisbee Daily Review 24, March 1902 page 1
"Fined $5 Each" Bisbee Daily Review 25, March 1902 page 8

French postcard showing a girl drinking from a glass water pitcher
c-1905

**Chase, Sydney:** She is believed to have worked at the Cora Miles house during 1902. Both Sydney and Grace Chase were arrested for assaulting Lillie Evans. Sydney was later acquitted of the crime.
"Cut with Water Pitcher" Bisbee Daily Review 24, March 1902 page 1
"Fined $5 Each" Bisbee Daily Review 25, March 1902 page 8

**Clark, Edna:** In 1909, she worked at No.33 Brewery Gulch. She was 28 years-old and from Atlanta, Georgia. Dora Tyson was listed as a friend. As of September 1909, she had been in Bisbee seven months.
Copper Queen Hospital Patients Register September 23, 1909 Bisbee Mining and Historical Museum, Bisbee.

**Clark, Fanny:** Operated the Casino in 1909.
Connell, C. T. (1909, April, 20). Untitled letter [Letter to Commissioner General of Immigration]. Office of Inspector in Charge, Douglas, Arizona.

**Collins, Atta:** She is suspected to have worked in the red-light district in 1900.

U.S. Census Bureau (1900). Bisbee, Arizona Territory, Cochise County District 0007,

**Compton, May:** This soiled dove was accused of theft in 1904.
"Jury Said Not Guilty" Bisbee Daily Review 21, April 1904 page 5

**Creason, Adine:** She tried to commit suicide by swallowing 30 tablets of *"corrosive sublimate."* (mercury dichloride) She left a suicide note that read *"Hell hath no fury like a woman scorned. Adine"* (Note, mercury dichloride was used to treat syphilis.)
"Attempts Suicide" Bisbee Daily Review 30, May 1916 page8

**Curenza, Jesus Miss:** This lady was arrested with Miss Manuwello Bustamante for violent intoxication, but the charges were dismissed. (Note, the name may be misspelled. It is written as in source)
"Warm Time in Tenderloin" Bisbee Daily Review 31, August 1904 page1

**Darnel, Edith:** In 1916, she was arrested for smuggling opium in a house owned by *"Monte Jack"* on Naco Road.
"Officers Raid Joint and Capture Opium Layout and Smokers" Bisbee Daily Review 19, October 1916 page 3
"Local Officers in Another Successful Raid on Opium Den" Bisbee Daily Review 20, 1916 page 8

**Davenport, May:** She had $2,000 in jewelry stolen from her while she was in a sanitarium in Phoenix.
"Jewelry Valued at $2,000 is Stolen" Bisbee Daily Review 8, May 1917 page 2

**Davis, Ruby:** Intoxicated at 11:00 PM on October 13, 1908, she asked, J.W. Smith to buy her a drink. He was passing her house No.128 and refused. She stabbed him in the chest with a knife almost killing him. Ruby was arrested and officers found drugs in the house.
"Girl Plunges Knife Close to Miner's Heart" Bisbee Daily Review 14, October 1908 page5

**Davison, Miss:** She was at the "Hog Ranch" when Ed Watts struck a miner named Andy Howard with a pick handle and knocked him down a flight of stone steps. She worked with Miss Wilson, Emma Voeltzel and Miss Lupe.
"Howard Hit with Pick Handle" Bisbee Daily Review 3, June 1902 page 1
"Howard Back" Bisbee Daily Review 10, January 1903 page 8

**Derowe, May:** Ms. Derowe was nearly killed when she was thrown from a horse on Naco Road. It was believed that her puffy hair style cushioned the impact and saved her. She worked at No.41 in 1906.
"Reckless Acts on Naco Road" Bisbee Daily Review 30, January 1906 page 5

**Desmon, Nora:** Trying to leave Bisbee, she forged a check supposedly written by Elmer Graham. Nora was arrested. She also, used the alias, Nellie Williams.
"Forged Graham's Name for $175" Bisbee Daily Review 16, December 1910 page 5

**Devoe, Vivian:** In 1913, she was 28-years-old and had lived in Bisbee four years. Originally, she came from Louisville, Kentucky. Marie Happe was her friend.
Copper Queen Hospital Patients Register December 6, 1913 Bisbee Mining and Historical Museum, Bisbee.

**Dodge, Clara E.:** She was about 23 years-old and worked in Bisbee for 2 ½ years in 1909. While working at No. 33 she drank a small bottle of carbolic acid and killed herself. Clara had a mother and two brothers in Denver Colorado and a sister in Manson (?) Iowa.
"Cochise County Coroner's Inquest #924" Arizona State Archives Phoenix

**Doe, Maude:** Fought with Allie Smith. She was arrested and fined $10.
"Woman Have Hair Pulling Scrimmage" Bisbee Daily Review 24 March 1910 page4

**Doyle, Della:** She worked at Bill Darr's place in 1906 and was arrested for stealing $20.00 from a miner who was drinking with her.
"Steals $20" Bisbee Daily Review 15, February1906 page7

**Dorthitt, Mary:** Operated a house in the red-light district in 1906. Her handyman John Tisdale, known locally as the *"Overall Kid"* was accused of vagrancy. Mary was born in the Indian Territory and in 1910 she was 31-years-old.

"Jury Finds Tisdale Guilty under the Vagrancy Law" Bisbee Daily Review 17, July 1906 page5
U.S. Census Bureau (1910). Bisbee Ward 1, Arizona Territory, Cochise County District 0005,

**Douthitt, May:** This African-American lady was arrested for smuggling cocaine, heroin, morphine and opium into Bisbee.
"Drug Ring is Bisbee Bared Two Arrested" Bisbee Daily Review 3, August 1919 page 3

**Douthitt, Viola:** Operated No. 41 in 1909. In 1910, she was listed as 41-years-old.
Connell, C. T. (1909, April, 20). Untitled letter [Letter to Commissioner General of Immigration]. Office of Inspector in Charge, Douglas, Arizona.

**Dowley, Jeanette:** In 1902, this girl emigrated from France. At 25 years-old in 1910 she was living in the red-light district with Marie Gusten.
U.S. Census Bureau (1910). Bisbee Ward 1, Arizona Territory, Cochise County District 0005

**Downs, Grace:** An ill-famed lady, who was accused of burglary, but the case was dismissed due to lack of witnesses.
"Town Tattle" The Arizona Daily Orb 15, July 1899 page 2

**Dunbar, Mollie:** See Dolly Dunbar

**Dunbar, Dolly:** On June 4, 1911, she attacked and wounded George Reardon with a corn razor. He needed 17 stitches to seal the wound. She was divorced by her husband, Thomas Dunbar for adultery in 1911. Note, her maiden name was Knapp and she was likely from Cananea, Sonora Mexico.
"Tries to Cut Throat of Guest" Bisbee Daily Review 6, June 1911 page 8
"Dunbar Case Before High Judge." Bisbee Daily Review 15, June 1911 page 5

"Mrs. Chaffins Gets Divorce Decree." Bisbee Daily Review 18, July 1911 page 8

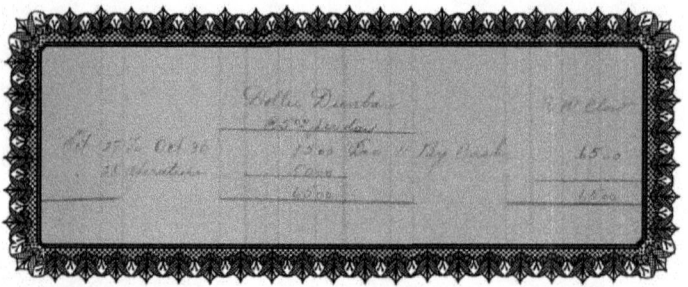

Hospital ledger showing payment of services by Dollie Dunbar, October 1911

**Duren, Rosa:** In 1908, she was arrested for working out of the district. The spelling of her name could have been Duran, but the newspaper has written it Duren.
"Woman to Jail" Bisbee Daily Review 7, June 1908 page 7

**Eades, Myrtle:** She was arrested with Pearl Eades in 1910 at the *"Manicure Parlor"* owned by N.M. Petty on O.K. Street. This house was operating illegally out of the red-light district.
"Woman Fined for Keeping Bad House" Bisbee Daily Review 22, July 1910 page 5

**Eades, Pearl:** Worked at the *"Manicure Parlor"* on O.K. Street in 1910. She was arrested for working out of district with Myrtle Eades.
"Woman Fined for Keeping Bad House" Bisbee Daily Review 22, July1910 page 5

**Eddie, Marie (Eddy):** Worked in house No. 41 Bisbee from 1906-1908.
"Miller is Bound over in Sum of $500" Bisbee Daily Review 11, August 1906 page 8
"Hearing Yesterday" Bisbee Daily Review 22, May 1908 page 7

**Elliott, L. A. Mrs.:** She was arrested for working as an ill-famed lady out of district at the Broadway Boarding House. Her fourteen-year-old son resided with her.
"Crusade Begins on Open Vice" Bisbee Daily Review 2, October 1910 page 4

**Ellison, Fay:** Remembered for hitting a man with a chair, while he was attacking Dolly Dunbar, Madam of House No.41 in 1906.
"Miller is Bound over in Sum of $500" Bisbee Daily Review 11, August 1906 page 8

**Encinas, Dora:** was arrested with Candelario Aguilar for operating an ill-famed house out of the redlight district.
"Bisbee News" Tombstone Prospector 7, October 1899 page 3

***"Estafina"*:** She was shot and wounded in a gun fight at Anita Romero's Place in 1900.
"Cochise County Coroner's Inquest #437" Arizona State Archives Phoenix

**Evans, Fannie:** The wife of Tom Evans, she was arrested for smuggling opium. She was arrested in a house owned by *"Monte Jack"* on Naco Road. Her husband was sentenced to one year in prison and she was released.
"Officers Raid Joint and Capture Opium Layout and Smokers" Bisbee Daily Review 19, October 1916 page 3
"Local Officers in Another Successful Raid on Opium Den" Bisbee Daily Review 20, 1916 page 8
"Sentenced to Prison" Bisbee Daily Review 22, November 1916 page 8

**Evans Lillie:** Believed to have worked for Cora Miles in 1902, she was struck with a water pitcher in a red-light brawl. Sydney and Grace Chase were blamed for striking her. Lillie was later fined $5.00 for her part of the fight.
"Cut with Water Pitcher" Bisbee Daily Review 24, March 1902 page 1
"Fined $5 Each" Bisbee Daily Review 25, March 1902 page 8

**Everett, Edna:** Worked in Bisbee around 1910 and possibly as early as 1908. In 1910, she was arrested by Constable McRae for disturbing the peace. After a horse ride to Lowell, she became disagreeable with residents of Naco Road.
"Edna Paid Ten" Bisbee Daily Review 10 February 1910 page 7

**Fawcett, Trixy:** This lady worked in Bisbee in 1906. She was attacked by Bert Welch in the Canadian Club.
"Bawdy House Row" Bisbee Daily Review 11, July 1906 page 5
"Trixy Fined $15" Bisbee Daily Review 6 December 1907 page 7

**Feilstan, Jessie:** She was arrested with Grace White for operating a house out of the red-light district and not having a license. Her bond

was paid for the property owner, Baptiste Caretto. Note, that Caretto owned a building that was partly inside the district and the other section was outside the red-light district. This was after the district limits were increased from 1,200 ft. from Central School to 1,300 ft. in 1906. Caretto had asked the city officials to place the structure entirely in the red-light district. Jessie may have been working out of this building.
"Bawdy House Keepers" Bisbee Daily Review 26, January 1906 page 1

**Fimbres Nellie:** An ill-famed Bisbee girl who was arrested in Douglas, Arizona just days after Bisbee's red-light district closed.
"Released on Bond" Bisbee Daily Review 11, December 1917 page 8

**Foster, Dot:** This 19-year-old was reported to have belonged to an important San Francisco family, but had become caught into the life of red-light girl. She was arrested in Bisbee on a warrant that she had stolen items from a house of ill-repute in Tucson. Kid Brown was arrested with her.
"Well Connected" Bisbee Daily Review 23, May 1906 page 5

**Fox, Thomas Mrs.:** Was arrested in 1905 for working out of the red-light district above the Butte Saloon.
"Butte House Trouble" Bisbee Daily Review 18, June 1905 page 1
"Mrs. Thos Fox is Found Guilty" Bisbee Daily Review 20, June 1905 page 5
"Justice Court Work in City" Bisbee Daily Review 21, June 1905 page 5

**Frush, Lena:** A feisty woman who was prone to fight, Worked in Bisbee in 1909 and became entangled in two fights in as many months. One with Helen Blanchard and the other with Millie Brown.
"Bisbee Courts Grind out Grist" Bisbee Daily Review 8, September1909 page 1
"Redlight Mixup is Finally Settled" Bisbee Daily Review 11, September1909 page 1
"Woman is Heavily Fined for Fight" Bisbee Daily Review 28, October 1909 page 8

**Fuss, Fredrick Mrs.:** The morning after her marriage to Fredrick Fuss, Mary Alice Fuss (Bacon) was arrested in 1903 and charged with operating an ill-famed house out of the red-light district at the Opera

Club house. Birdie Russell and Grace Martin were arrested and plead guilty. After a trial Mrs. Fuss was acquitted.
"Lewd Women Arrested" Bisbee Daily Review 26, February 1903 page 4
"Mrs. Fuss is Acquitted" Bisbee Daily Review 27, February 1903 page 8

**Gales, Mary:** A girl of the red-light district at Brewery Gulch. She was arrested for disturbing the peace in Lowell.
"Got too Obnoxious" Bisbee Daily Review 11, December 1907 page 3

**Gallagher, Bridget:** Originally, from Kiel, Mays County, Ireland this 22-year-old had been in Bisbee only six weeks when she committed suicide by drinking Phenol/ Lysol. She was survived by her parents Anthony and Mary Gallagher in Kiel, Ireland. Ms. Gallagher was buried in Evergreen Cemetery at Bisbee.
Copper Queen Hospital Patients Register May 24, 1914 Bisbee Mining and Historical Museum, Bisbee.
"Original Certificate of Death." Arizona Department of Health
http://genealogy.az.gov/azdeath/085/10850056.pdf (August, 16 2015)

**Garnett, Dora:** A madam that shot and killed another madam Irene Logan in 1899. In 1901, she was a primary witness in the death of Oscar Young.
"Cochise County Coroner's Inquest #9" Arizona State Archives Phoenix

**Geary, Mary:** This madam operated the Hog Ranch in Brewery Gulch from about 1897, until at least 1901. Mary was born in Missouri in May of 1861.
"Cochise County Coroner's Inquest #4" Arizona State Archives Phoenix
U.S. Census Bureau (1900). Bisbee, Arizona Territory, Cochise County District 0007,

**Gibson, Jane:** She was arrested for fighting with Alice Pierce. After being arrested she drank poison.
"Young Girl Tries to Take Life" Bisbee Daily Review 12, September 1912 page 3

**Gibson, Mrs.:** Arrested, when the Norton House was raided for prostitution in 1906.
"House is Raided" Bisbee Daily Review 11, April 1906 page 8
"Norton House" Bisbee Daily Review 12, April 1906 page 5

**Gibson, Phillis:** This woman is most likely actually Phyllis Sherwood and the name Phillis Gibson was written up by the newspaper by mistake.

"Last Round in Fight" Bisbee Daily Review 6, August 1903 page 5
"Cora Miles Arrested" Bisbee Daily Review 11, August 1903 page 5
"It is A Felonious Charge" Bisbee Daily Review 15, August 1903 page 5
"Cora Miles Dismissed" Bisbee Daily Review 16, August 1903 page 5

**Gilliland, Gladys:** This lady worked at the Shea House in Lowell in 1906. She was mistakenly arrested for stealing $40, but it was later revealed the suspect was actually Gladys Schwartz of the People's Theater.

"To be tried for Picking Pocket" Bisbee Daily Review 24, March 1906 page 5

**Gilliland, Margarete (Margaret?):** Pressed charges against police officer C.C. McCoy for disturbing the peace and having a gun while drunk.

"Officer McCoy Fined" Bisbee Daily Review 29, April 1908 page 7
"Charge against McCoy" Bisbee Daily Review 8, May 1908 page 7

**Gillis, May:** Ms. Gillis worked at No.9 Brewery Gulch in 1907 and had lived in the United States three years. She was from Ireland and her parents are recorded as Mike McGourty and Rose McGourty.

Copper Queen Hospital Patients Register August 23, 1907 Bisbee Mining and Historical Museum, Bisbee.
"Raid House that is Near School" Bisbee Daily Review 23, April 1912 page 8

**Gordon, Kate:** See Mrs. Kate Savage

**Gray, *"Blonde Josie"*:** In 1906, she tried to commit suicide by drinking carbolic acid.

"Attempt not Successful" Bisbee Daily Review 13, September 1906 page 3

**Greer, Fay:** Ms. Greer became entangled in a fight with Hester Parker, Charles King and J.M. Davis in 1912.

"Tenderloin Fight" Bisbee Daily Review 27 April 1912 page 3

**Gusten, Marie:** She was arrested in 1909 for fighting with another tenderloin girl, Hester Parker. Marie was 21-years-old in 1910 and was born in Texas.
"Women Pull Hair Then Pay Fine" Bisbee Daily Review 17, December 1909 page 8
U.S. Census Bureau (1910). Bisbee Ward 1, Arizona Territory, Cochise County District 0005

**Hall, Lillie:** In 1905, she was arrested for being drunk and disorderly. Although, there is no positive identification she was a woman of the red-light she was considered a *"Lewd"* woman.
"Lowell Morality Move" Bisbee Daily Review 21, February 1905 page 5

**Happe, Marie:** This German, woman was arrested for threatening the life of Hester Parker another lady of the red-light in 1911. She was fined $25. In 1900, Marie emigrated from Germany. Marie was 23-years-old in 1910.
"Hate and Disorder in the Tenderloin" Bisbee Daily Review 7, May 1911 page 8
"Wholesale Arrests" Bisbee Daily Review 18, June 1912 page 6
U.S. Census Bureau (1910). Bisbee Ward 1, Arizona Territory, Cochise County District 0005,

**Hartinan, Emma:** She worked at No.9 Brewery Gulch in 1907 and was a friend of May Gillis.
Copper Queen Hospital Patients Register August 23, 1907 Bisbee Mining and Historical Museum, Bisbee.

**Hash, Lulu:** A native of Illinois, this 26-year-old worked with Dora Tyson.
U.S. Census Bureau (1910). Bisbee, Ward 1 Arizona Territory, Cochise County District 0005,

**Hastings, Mabel:** Operated an ill-famed house in Brewery Gulch in 1903. Mabel was the daughter of Minnie Carey
"Officers have in Custody Men Supposed Murdered L.O. Milless" Bisbee Daily Review 1, October 1903 page 1
"Cochise County Coroner's Inquest #114" Arizona State Archives Phoenix

**Hight, Bessie:** This red-light girl was arrested with Mary Moore by Constable Doyle at the Beer Garden in Johnson Addition.

 115

"Trouble at the Beer Garden" Bisbee Daily Review 16, July 1902 page 1

**Highwarton, Rosie:** Attacked Madam, Lee Watson with a knife. She was reported to be of mixed Native American, White and African-American descent.
"Savage Attempt to Murder is Charged" Bisbee Daily Review 28, April 1907 page 5
"Bound Over to Await Action of Grand Jury" Bisbee Daily Review 1, May 1907 page 8

**Holt, Dora Mrs.:** This soiled dove was arrested for defrauding a resident for $18.00.
"Dora out of Trouble" Bisbee Daily Review 4, December 1902 page 8

**Hooper, Annie Mrs.:** She was arrested for running a disorderly house in Lowell in September 1907. The day after being released she returned to the Bisbee jail and married J.H. Brown. This young man had been arrested for living at her ill-famed house. Mrs. Hooper is likely the same person as Mrs. S.A. Hooper.
"Versatile Frijoles Gave Away Bride" Bisbee Evening Miner 12, September 1907 page 5
"Wedding Services Performed in Jail" Bisbee Daily Review 12, September 1907 page 5

**Hooper, S.A. Mrs.:** She is possibly an ill-famed lady. In the 1907, Mrs. Hooper was arrested for being a *"Lewd and dissolute person"* in a tent on the John Daisy mining claim near Lowell. Note, Mrs. Annie Hooper is likely the same person.
"Price Arrested as Vagrant in Lowell" Bisbee Daily Review 23, August 1907 page 3

**Howard, Francis:** Arrested for *"visiting"* a man at the Lockie House. She was fined $7.50.
"In City Court" Bisbee Daily Review 31, January 1914 page 6

**Howard, Lillian:** See Lillian Shea

**Howe, Peggy:** This girl possibly worked in the district. She went for help when a fight broke out between Marie Gusten and Hester Parker.
"Women Pull Hair Then Pay Fine" Bisbee Daily Review 17, December 1909 page 8

**Hudson, Emma:** This lady worked at the Hog Ranch in 1901.
"Cochise County Coroner's Inquest #4" Arizona State Archives Phoenix

**Humphreys, Opal:** Left, Bisbee to work in the cabarets at Nogales, Sonora.
"Girls Arrests Leads to Probe by U.S. Agents." Bisbee Daily Review 28, March 1922 page 8

**Hunt, Maud:** Worked at No. 9 Brewery Gulch under Marie Happe.
"Cochise County Coroner's Inquest #870" Arizona State Archives Phoenix

**Hunter Bell:** She was arrested and accused of working out of the red-light district. Bell was reportedly too ill to attend her trial.
"Lewd Women Arrested" Bisbee Daily Review 26, February 1903 page 4
"Mrs. Fuss is Acquitted" Bisbee Daily Review 27, February 1903 page 8

**Hurbert, Camelhi:** At 30 years old, she worked in Bisbee in 1913 and originally came from New Mexico. Her father's name is believed to be Baltiari Auciou.
Copper Queen Hospital Patients Register August 12, 1913 Bisbee Mining and Historical Museum, Bisbee.

**Ikner, Pearl:** A few days, after leaving Bisbee, Pearl shot and killed Hiram Smith in Douglas, Arizona.
"Cochise County Coroner's Inquest #439" Arizona State Archives Phoenix

**James, Maud:** Attempted to commit suicide by taking creolin. Two women saved her. Reportedly, she had offered the cup containing the poison to a man that later visited her as she was being treated.
"Swallows Poison in Effort to End Life" Bisbee Daily Review 5, November 1910 page 4

**Jensen, Molly:** During 1912, she was arrested for fighting in the red-light district. Both Molly and Mae Scott were arrested for *"being participants in the glass and head breaking affair."* The night police officer was not on duty when the fight occurred.
"Tough Tenderloin is Hailed into Court" Bisbee Daily Review 14, March 1912 page 6

**Jerome, May:** Was hit by a man at House No.41 in 1906.
"Hit Woman" Bisbee Daily Review 20, March 1906 page 6

**Joe, Jennie:** This woman was arrested for pointing a revolver at a drunken, James Welsh.
"Rough House in Red Light on Trial Today" <u>Bisbee Evening Miner</u> 4, September 1907 page 1

**Johnson, Henrietta:** She was arrested in the district for violating Prohibition.
"Two Women Charged with Having Booze" <u>Bisbee Daily Review</u> 1, June 1917page 5

**Johnson, Josie:** Worked at No.27 Brewery Gulch under Con Shea in 1905.
"Cochise County Coroner's Inquest #244" Arizona State Archives Phoenix

**King, Mrs.:** This lady was only in Bisbee a few days. She registered at the Copper Queen Hotel as Mrs. King from San Francisco, but after three days the hotel asked her to leave because of her poor choice of companions. After leaving the hotel she took a room in the red-light district then she took a train to El Paso. She was suspect in the murder of a bank clerk named, J.F. Harrell. It was thought she may be the elusive *"Minnie"* that had written Harrell numerous letters.
"Harrell Murder Mystery slowly being Worked out-New links in case" <u>Bisbee Daily Review</u> 14, May 1914 page 1

**Kline, Sadie:** Suspected of being an ill-famed lady. She associated with A.A. Rosenwald.
Connell, C. T. (1909, June 14, 1909). No. 32A [Letter to Thos. M. Fisher jr.]. Office of Inspector in Charge, Douglas, Arizona.

**LaVerne, Sybil:** She was arrested for stealing $575 from Bert Noftz with Phyllis Sherwood. The case was later dismissed.
"Cora Miles Arrested" <u>Bisbee Daily Review</u> 11, August 1903 page 5
"It is A Felonious Charge" <u>Bisbee Daily Review</u> 15, August 1903 page 5
"Cora Miles Dismissed" <u>Bisbee Daily Review</u> 16, August 1903 page 5
"Women are in Jail" <u>Bisbee Daily Review</u> 16, August 1903 page 5
"Case Against Women Dismissed" <u>Bisbee Daily Review</u> 18, August 1903 page 5

**Layman, Myrie:** This woman worked in the district during 1910 and unsuccessfully tried to commit suicide. She had a husband reported to be living in Naco.
"Attempts Suicide" <u>Bisbee Daily Review</u> 18, October 1910 page 5

**Layral, Gabrielle:** See Marguerite Lefebvre

**Laws, Mattie:** In 1906, she arrested with Ethel Scott in a drunken brawl.
"Negroes Fight" Bisbee Daily Review 4, May 1906 page 5

**Lefebvre, Marguerite:** Described as slender and tiny, being only 5 ft. tall. Marguerite was delicate and pretty and operated the Canadian Club. She spoke broken English with a French accent and was about 20 years-old in 1909. Her real name may have been Gabrielle Layral.
Connell, C. T. (1909, April, 20). Untitled letter [Letter to Commissioner General of Immigration]. Office of Inspector in Charge, Douglas, Arizona.
Connell, C. T. (1909, July, 15). No. 32A [Letter to A. de la Torre]. Office of Inspector in Charge, Douglas, Arizona.

**LeGrand, Angie:** She was the *"Mistress"* at a red-light house called the Casino in 1906. After drinking heavily one night, she tried to pull out the money drawer and a pistol fell. The weapon fired and a bullet struck Mistress LeGrand in the right arm. She was not fatally injured.
"Red-light Lady Shoots Herself" Bisbee Daily Review 11, March 1906 page 5

**Levoie, Annie:** Operated a saloon in the red-light district during 1906. Very likely also had girls working from the saloon.
"Change of Venue in Tenderloin Case" Bisbee Daily Review 2, June 1906 page 6

**Lewis, Dollie:** This girl lived at No.41 and was a witness in the death of Minnie Carey.
"Cochise County Coroner's Inquest #114" Arizona State Archives Phoenix

**Lopez, Victoria:** She was born in 1876 in Mexico and immigrated to the United States in 1899. Victoria worked with Anita Romero.
U.S. Census Bureau (1900). Bisbee, Arizona Territory, Cochise County District 0007,

**Lupe, Miss:** She was at the "Hog Ranch" when Ed Watts struck a miner named Andy Howard with a pick handle and knocked him

down a flight of stone steps. She worked with Miss Davison, Miss Wilson and Emma Voeltzel
"Howard Hit with Pick Handle" Bisbee Daily Review 3, June 1902 page 1
"Howard Back" Bisbee Daily Review 10, January 1903 page 8

**Lusk, Lottie:** A red-light lady who was arrested for disturbing the peace and fined $25.
"On the War Path" Bisbee Daily Review 20, October, 1910 page 5

**Mabry, Kathryn Mrs.:** Convicted of trying to lure underage girls into an immoral lifestyle.
"Girls Tell Story of Revolting Crime and Carousals" Bisbee Daily Review 10, December 1909 page 1
"Girls Tell Story of Revolting Crime" Bisbee Daily Review 10, December 1909 page 8
"House on School Hill Holds Girls as Prisoners" Bisbee Daily Review 11, December 1909 page 1
"Court Hears Mabry Case and Finds Woman Guilty" Bisbee Daily Review 14, December 1909 page 8
"Taken to Hospital" Bisbee Daily Review 15, January 1910 page 8

**Mahon Elsie:** In 1909, she was accused of stealing $40.00 from a man. She resided in Ruby-Glim row in Brewery Gulch.
"Elsie's Case Postponed" Bisbee Daily Review 14, December 1909 page 9

**Major, Mrs.:** Arrested at the Norton House for working out of the red-light district in 1906.
"House is Raided" Bisbee Daily Review 11, April 1906 page 8
"Norton House" Bisbee Daily Review 1, April 1906 page 5

**Malcom, Lily:** Worked at house No.41 in 1906 and was called as a witness in an assault case.
"Miller is Bound over in Sum of $500" Bisbee Daily Review 11, August 1906 page 8

**Maloney, Mrs.:** This lady was arrested for working out of the red-light district at the Norton House in 1906.
"House is Raided" Bisbee Daily Review 11, April 1906 page 8
"Norton House" Bisbee Daily Review 12, April 1906 page 5

**Maritiana, Inez:** An ill-famed lady, who cut Adolph Bohn.
"Copperings" Tombstone Epitaph 20, August 1899 page 2

**Martin, Blanche:** She worked at No. 41 in 1905.

"Mrs. Thos Fox is Found Guilty" <u>Bisbee Daily Review</u> 20, June 1905 page 5

**Martin, Grace:** She was arrested in 1903 with Birdie Russell, Mrs. Fredrick Fuss and Bell Hunter for working out of the red-light district at the Opera Club House. Rather than go to trial, she plead guilty.
"Lewd Women Arrested" <u>Bisbee Daily Review</u> 26, February 1903 page 4
"Mrs. Fuss is Acquitted" <u>Bisbee Daily Review</u> 27, February 1903 page 8

**Marvin, Florence Mrs.:** Mrs. Marvin worked at No.33 Brewery Gulch. In November 1909 at 22 years-old, she came down with typhoid. Originally, she came from Bukfield, Missouri (Brookfield?) and her parents were J.E. Curtis and Martha Curtis. She had been in Bisbee only three weeks when she became ill. On December 7, 1909 she was released from the hospital. In 1910, she was extradited to Texas to face perjury charges in a bank robbing case.
Copper Queen Hospital Patients Register November 25, 1909 Bisbee Mining and Historical Museum, Bisbee.
"Texas Sheriff is Here for Prisoner" <u>Bisbee Daily Review</u> 10, March 1910 page 8

**Mattie, Miss:** She was as arrested with a Miss Trixy for drunk and disorderly conduct behind the Annex Saloon. Mattie was fined $15.00 after pleading guilty
"Ladies Arrested" <u>Bisbee Daily Review</u> 10, January 1903 page 8
"Paid $15" <u>Bisbee Daily Review</u> 11, January 1903 page 8

**Mattison, Katie:** Reportedly in 1905, she assaulted another ill-famed girl and then fled to Douglas, Arizona.
"Brought Woman Back" <u>Bisbee Daily Review</u> 15, February 1905 page 6

**May, Edna:** This girl was arrested for disturbing the peace in 1912 and fined $10.00.
"Reflection Brings Plea" <u>Bisbee Daily Review</u> 1, March 1912 page 3

**Mayfield, Mildred:** A girl in the red-light district. She died in Tombstone in 1907.
"Downward Path Leads to Death" <u>Bisbee Daily Review</u> 10, November 1907 page 1

**McCoy, Alma:** Attempted suicide in 1917 by taking mercury dichloride tablets. (Mercury dichloride was used to treat syphilis)
"Swallows Bichloride of Mercury Tablets in Despondency Fit" Bisbee Daily Review 10, March 1917 page 8

**McGowan, Ms.:** See Mrs. Thomas Fox

**McHenry, Helen:** This woman operated an ill-famed house in 1907. At this time, she was caught selling alcohol without a license.
"Caught Selling Liquor, had no License" Bisbee Daily Review 30, August 1907 page 5

**Mehon, Elsie:** She was accused of stealing $40 from a client.
"Trip to Red Light Gets Court Airing" Bisbee Daily Review 12, December 1909 page 7

**"Midget":** A red-light girl who was arrested for disturbing the peace.
"Fine $20" Bisbee Daily Review 24, April 1908 page 7

**Miles, Cora:** A woman who often found herself in difficulties. Cora operated a house on Brewery Gulch in 1903-1904. This lady was accused of using opium and trying to stab another Phyllis Sherwood with an ice pick. She was later known as Cora Wortman.
"Cora Miles Arrested" Bisbee Daily Review 11, August 1903 page 5
"It is A Felonious Charge" Bisbee Daily Review 15, August 1903 page 5
"Cora Miles Dismissed" Bisbee Daily Review 16, August 1903 page 5
"Women are in Jail" Bisbee Daily Review 16, August 1903 page 5
"Case Against Women Dismissed" Bisbee Daily Review 18, August 1903 page 5
"A Muddled Charge Dismissed" Bisbee Daily Review 4, September 1903 page 5
"Hop-Layout Found in House of Ill-Fame." Bisbee Daily Review 4, September 1903 page 1
"Change of Venue in Tenderloin Case." Bisbee Daily Review 2, June 1906 page 6

**Miller Andy J. Mrs.:** Operated No.41 in 1909. She became entangled with the law after 16-year-old Lillie Neatherlin began working for her. Mrs. Miller was accused of enticing Lillie to work at her house and forcing her to stay.
"Courtroom Looks Like House Party" Bisbee Daily Review 23, December 1909 page 3

**Miller, Emma:** A native of Texas, Emma worked with Dora Tyson. She was 27-years-old in 1910. U.S. Census Bureau (1910). Bisbee, Ward 1 Arizona Territory, Cochise County District 0005,

**Miller, Rose:** Operated a house in Brewery Gulch in 1901.
"Cochise County Coroner's Inquest #4" Arizona State Archives Phoenix

**Monbar, Dolly:** The same woman known as Dolly Dunbar.

**Moore, Bertha:** Her home in the red-light district was burglarized in 1907.
"Young Boys are Charged with Burglary" Bisbee Daily Review 2, February 1907 page 8

**Moore, Mary:** This lady of the night was arrested with Bessie Hight by Constable Doyle at the Beer Garden. "Trouble at the Beer Garden" Bisbee Daily Review 16, July 1902 page 1

**Neatherlin, Della:** Left home to enter house No. 41. Later, she convinced her 16-year-old sis Lillian to join her. Della married Arthur McKerracher.
Courtroom Looks Like House Party" Bisbee Daily Review 23, December 1909 page 3
"No. 41 Proves Trap for Girl" Bisbee Daily Review 19, December 1909 page 1
Harnessmaker gets it Tangle" Bisbee Daily Review 18, December 1909 page 8

**Neatherlin, Lillian:** A 16-year-old that entered No 41 on Brewery Gulch. Since she was under age the madam Mrs. Andy Miller was arrested.
Courtroom Looks Like House Party" Bisbee Daily Review 2, December 1909 page 3
"No. 41 Proves Trap for Girl" Bisbee Daily Review 19, December 1909 page 1

**Neill, Ethel:** A Bisbee ill-famed girl. She was beaten by up by a man in Naco at the Cow Ranch Saloon in 1908.
"Pete Cook Gets What He Needs" Bisbee Daily Review 18, September 1908 page 5

**Norton, May:** A lady from No. 33, She was arrested for stealing $125.00 from a man. May refused to provide bail and remained in jail.

123

"Woman is Arrested for Robbery of Man" Bisbee Daily Review 8, April 1906 page 1

**Parker, Hester:** Ready and willing to fight, in 1909 Hester engaged Marie Gusten in a brawl. Later, she was arrested along with Marie Happe, Tempest Wyland and Dora Tyson in a red-light brawl that occurred on the night of May 5, 1911. Hester filed the complaint that resulted in Marie Happe being arrested. The trouble, continued, when in June 13, 1911 her husband, Frank Hayward ran off with Mae Scott another tenderloin girl and was arrested for firing a shot at him and threatening to kill him. In 1911, she had a six-year-old son.
"Women Pull Hair Then Pay Fine" Bisbee Daily Review 17, December 1909 page 8
"Hate and Disorder in the Tenderloin" Bisbee Daily Review 7, May 1911 page 8
"Jealous Woman Goes After Husband and Tries to Kill Him" Bisbee Daily Review 15, June 1911 page 8
"Parker Woman is Freed by Court" Bisbee Daily Review 18, June 1911 page 8

**Paterson, Ethel:** Worked at No.9 in Brewery Gulch then operated by Marie Happe in 1911. She had worked in Bisbee for close to one year, when she drank a small bottle of carbolic acid and killed herself. Her mother had predeceased her, but she was survived by a four-year-old child and her father, Joe R. Clough.
"Cochise County Coroner's Inquest #870" Arizona State Archives Phoenix

**Pearson, Mrs. (Mabel):** See Mabel Carlise

**Peck, Ida:** Fined when she accidently fired a gun while toying with it in her room.
"Woman is Fined" Bisbee Daily Review 6, February 1907 page 7

**Pennington, Eunice:** In 1909, she worked at No.33 in Brewery Gulch and one of the last people to see Clara Dodge alive. Eunice was 23-years-old in 1910 and from Texas.
"Cochise County Coroner's Inquest #924" Arizona State Archives Phoenix
U.S. Census Bureau (1910). Bisbee Ward 1, Arizona Territory, Cochise County District 0005

**Phillips, Pearl:** In 1903, this lady was working at the Cora Miles House and was accused of stealing a watch.
"A Muddled Charge Dismissed" Bisbee Daily Review 4, September 1903 page 5

**Pierce, Alice:** She fought with Jane Gibson and was arrested.
"Young Girl Tries to Take Life" Bisbee Daily Review 12, September 1912 page 3

**Prather, Emma:** In 1901, she worked at the Hog Ranch. Emma had been in Bisbee around four months in 1901. She had come from Osborn, New Mexico, where she had been a cook.
"Cochise County Coroner's Inquest #4" Arizona State Archives Phoenix

**Ray, Mildred:** See Mrs. Kate Savage

**Raymond, Rubie:** Worked in Bisbee in 1907 and became sick with typhoid fever.
"Stole Money Given to Unfortunate Woman" Bisbee Daily Review 4, June 1907 page 5

**"Red Jean":** Described as a striking yet physically powerful red-headed *"hell-cat"* and compared to the Roman goddess, Juno.
Chisholm, Joe. *Brewery Gulch*. San Antonio: Naylor, 1949. Print.

**Reed, (?):** This girl was arrested in Lowell, Arizona for vagrancy. She was unable to prove she had respectable employment. Previous she had worked in the red-light district in Brewery Gulch.
"Undesirables are Given Jail Terms" Bisbee Daily Review 12, November 1910 page 8

**Reese, Helen:** Worked in the district in 1914 and was the sister of Rita Reese.
"Despondent Rita Reese Ends Life by Taking Poison" Bisbee Daily Review 15, August 1914 page 3

**Reese, Rita:** She committed suicide in 1914 by drinking carbolic acid. She was the sister of Helen Reese.
"Despondent Rita Reese Ends Life by Taking Poison" Bisbee Daily Review 15, August 1914 page 3

**Rice, Julia:** This African-American girl was born in Tennessee during 1877. She worked with Mary Geary.
U.S. Census Bureau (1900). Bisbee, Arizona Territory, Cochise County District 0007,

**Robertson, Tidy:** Worked in the district in 1906. She attacked Ethel Scott with a rock during a drunken brawl.
"Negroes Fight" Bisbee Daily Review 4, May 1906 page 5

**Robinson, Mabel:** She is suspected to have worked in the red-light district in 1900.
U.S. Census Bureau (1900). Bisbee, Arizona Territory, Cochise County District 0007,

**Romero, Anita:** Operated, a wild house starting in 1899. She was originally from southern Mexico. She was born in January 1875.
Chisholm, Joe. *Brewery Gulch*. San Antonio: Naylor, 1949. Print.
"Cochise County Coroner's Inquest #437" Arizona State Archives Phoenix
"Cochise County Coroner's Inquest of Rosario Tapeta, December 18, 1900" Arizona State Archives Phoenix
U.S. Census Bureau (1900). Bisbee, Arizona Territory, Cochise County District 0007,

**Romero, Lucio (Lucia sp?):** She tried to break out the one-legged gambler, Arthur Finney out of jail. After he stabbed Guillermo Romero in an ill-famed house. She was sentenced to 190 days in jail or a pay a $190.00 fine. It is not clear if, she was the girl working at the Julius Cardinas Place that the two men were fighting over.
"All Over Arizona" The Arizona Republic 28, September 1897 page 4

**Romero, Petra:** Worked the Little Casino and witnessed the murder of 17- year-old William Phillips.
"Cochise County Coroner's Inquest #236" Arizona State Archives Phoenix

**Roseman, Fannie:** In 1908, she became entangled with trouble after shooting at two men. One of which was a drunken Dr. Cassady.
"Ugly Row in Tenderloin" Bisbee Daily Review 18, April 1908 page 5

***"Roxie":*** an African American ill-famed lady who had $700.00 in jewelry stolen from her. It was recovered by City Marshal Basset Watkins.
"Missing Jewels Returned" Bisbee Daily Review 25, September 1910 page 5

**Rosenwald, Ida:** Suspected to be an ill-famed lady associated with A.A. Rosenwald.
Connell, C. T. (1909, June 14, 1909). No. 32A [Letter to Thos. M. Fisher jr.]. Office of Inspector in Charge, Douglas, Arizona.

**Russell, Birdie:** In 1903, she was arrested with Grace Martin, Mrs. Fredrick Fuss and Bell Hunter for working out of the red-light district at the Opera Club House. She plead guilty to the charges.
"Lewd Women Arrested" Bisbee Daily Review 26, February 1903 page 4
"Mrs. Fuss is Acquitted" Bisbee Daily Review 27, February 1903 page 8

**Sanpey, Amelia:** Worked in red-light district for one month before moving to Aqua Prieta, Mexico to work.
"Take Desperado and Woman on Federal Charge, After Urgent Washington Wire. Bisbee Daily Review 13, February 1914 page 1

**Saathoff, Lillie:** Was arrested for leaving Bisbee to work in cabarets at Nogales, Sonora.
"Girls Arrests Leads to Probe by U.S. Agents." Bisbee Daily Review 28, March 1922 page 8

**Savage, Kate Mrs.:** She came to Bisbee from Colorado, around 1903 with her husband Henry Savage. Kate worked as a mistress at a house of ill-fame under the name of Mildred Ray. In 1905, Kate and her son Amos Stone ambushed and killed Mr. Savage in Tombstone Canyon.
"Killed Her Husband. Bisbee Daily Review 4, August 1905 page 1
"Murderess Rejoices in Terrible Work. Bisbee Daily Review 4, August 1905 page 8

**Schwartz, Gladys:** Employed at the People's Theater in 1906 and was arrested for stealing two $20 gold pieces from Walter Button.
"To be tried for Picking Pocket" Bisbee Daily Review 24, March 1906 page 5

**Scott, Ethel:** Worked the district in 1906. She was attacked with a rock by Tidy Robertson in a brawl.
"Negroes Fight" Bisbee Daily Review 4, May 1906 page 5

**Scott, Mae:** During 1912, she was arrested for fighting in the red-light district. Both Mae and Molly Jensen were arrested for *"being participants in the glass and head breaking affair."* She was the same, Mae Scott that placed an ad in the newspaper absolving herself of any debts of Frank Hayward. Mae was originally, from Virginia and in 1910 was 26-years-old.
"Tough Tenderloin is Hailed into Court" Bisbee Daily Review 14, March 1912 page 6
U.S. Census Bureau (1910). Bisbee, Ward 1 Arizona Territory, Cochise County District 0005,

**Sharp, Florence:** One of the last of the madams of the legal era. She was arrested for disturbing the peace and fined $25.00, but she harassed police officers in the district and was fined $75.00 or 75 days in jail on April 3, 1917.
"Dairyman is Fined $50 in City Court After Many Delays" Bisbee Daily Review 4, April 1917page 5

**Shea, Lillian *"Lillie"*:** Also, known as Lillie Howard operated with her husband Con Shea, No. 27 in Brewery Gulch. In 1906, they moved their ill-famed house outside of Lowell. She had a violently abusive relationship with her husband.
"Con Shay is Found Guilty" Bisbee Daily Review 2, March 1904 page 5

**Shepard, Alethea:** She worked with Irene Brown and came from Texas. In 1910, she was 35-years-old.
U.S. Census Bureau (1910). Bisbee, Ward 1 Arizona Territory, Cochise County District 0005,

**Sheriff, Ethel:** This lady lived in Bisbee for a short time in 1902. She came to Bisbee with a man named Shelby Parker, whom she married in Bisbee. Her mother came to Bisbee and the three of them took up temporary residence in two adobe rooms behind no.41 in the red-light district.
"City Police Arrest Parker" Bisbee Daily Review 30, September 1902 page 8

**Sherwood, Phyllis:** She worked at the Cora Miles House in 1903 and accused Cora of trying to kill her with an ice pick. Later, Cora accused her and Sybil LaVerne of stealing $575 from Bert Nofts.
"Cora Miles Arrested" Bisbee Daily Review 11, August 1903 page 5
"It is A Felonious Charge" Bisbee Daily Review 15, August 1903 page 5
"Cora Miles Dismissed" Bisbee Daily Review 16, August 1903 page 5
"Women are in Jail" Bisbee Daily Review 16, August 1903 page 5
"Case Against Women Dismissed" Bisbee Daily Review 18, August 1903 page 5

**Silver, Lily:** A 19-year-old French girl that was deported back to France once, then returned to Bisbee via Canada. The second time she was arrested to be deported was in 1908. A young Bisbee man offered to marry her, so she could remain in the United States.
"Would Marry French Girl to Save Her" Bisbee Daily Review 12, July 1908 page 5

**Smith, Allie:** Joined a hair-pulling fight with Maude Doe in 1910.
"Woman Have Hair Pulling Scrimmage" Bisbee Daily Review 24, March 1910 page 4

**Smith, Mrs.:** She was arrested for running a house of prostitution in the Norton House on Main Street, out of the red-light district. The legitimate houses in the red-light district had complained that Mrs. Smith operation was not paying the red-light taxes, like the legal houses.
"House is Raided" Bisbee Daily Review 11, April 1906 page 8
"Norton House" Bisbee Daily Review 12, April 1906 page 5

**Smith, Myrtle:** In 1914, she was 22 years-old and had lived in Bisbee one year. Originally, she had come from Hain, Montana. On February 24, 1914 she was hospitalized for *"morphinism"*. She listed a Mrs. Miller in San Mateo, California as her friend.
Copper Queen Hospital Patients Register February 24, 1914 Bisbee Mining and Historical Museum, Bisbee.

**Sommers, Carrie:** During 1904, she accidently swallowed a significant amount of Laudanum. Ms. Sommers had mistaken it for cough syrup.
"Poison by Mistake" Bisbee Daily Review 4, September 1904 page 5

**Sonoqui, Octaviana:** This woman was deported at least three times. She entered the country to work as an ill-famed lady. This was grounds for deportation. Octaviana was jailed in Lowell, before being sent to Tucson for deportation proceedings.
"Will be Deported" Bisbee Daily Review 7, June 1908 page 7

**St Clair, Dollie:** She was arrested at the Ozark Rooming House in 1916 for opium. A man named George Warren was also arrested.
"Local; Officers in Another Successful Raid on Opium Den" Bisbee Daily Review 20, October 1916 page 8

**Stanley, Ruth:** Worked at No.9 Brewery Gulch in 1908. She was 31 years old and had lived in Cochise County three years.
Copper Queen Hospital Patients Register January 28, 1908 Bisbee Mining and Historical Museum, Bisbee.

**Stewart, Maryland:** Worked in Bisbee in 1907 and took a fatal dose of poison, while drunk. It appeared she was going to survive, but she later died. Her body was shipped for burial in Memphis, Tennessee by an uncle.
"Will Probably Recover" Bisbee Daily Review 30, November 1907 page 5
"Poison Proves Fatal" Bisbee Daily Review 1, December 1907 page 5
"Corpse Sent Today" Bisbee Daily Review 6, December 1907 page 5

**Straum, Grace Mrs.:** Abandoned by her husband, she died from pneumonia in a room at the Little Casino in 1906. Her husband was in Fort Scott, Kansas and refused to pay for her funeral. Straum's parents were reported to be Mr. and Mrs. Baldwin in Pleasanton, Kansas.
"Sorrows at End" Bisbee Daily Review 26, June1906 page 5

**Taylor, Harriet:** Her husband was accused of prostituting her near Johnson Addition at the Beer Garden.
"Takes Taylor Case under Advisement" Bisbee Daily Review 2, May 1909 page 8

**Tichenor, Helen:** After falling from a porch of a red-light house, she was taken to the Copper Queen Hospital at 5:30 am on the 4th of July 1909. It was determined she had a fractured skull. Her condition worsened and she died on July 5th. Ms. Tichenor was from Evansville, Illinois and her mother's name was Mrs. T.M. Rothrock. It is likely, she worked for Dora Tyson, who is listed as her friend.
Copper Queen Hospital Patients Register July 4, 1909 Bisbee Mining and Historical Museum, Bisbee.
"Minor Injuries" Bisbee Daily Review 9, July 1909 page 7

**Thomas, Edna:** A native of Texas, Edna worked with Dora Tyson. She was 30 years-old in 1910.
U.S. Census Bureau (1910). Bisbee, Ward 1 Arizona Territory, Cochise County District 0005,

**Thompson, Georgia:** She is suspected of working in the red-light district in 1910. Georgia lived with Viola Douhitt
U.S. Census Bureau (1910). Bisbee, Ward 1 Arizona Territory, Cochise County District 0005,

**Tomkins, Myrtle:** A red-light girl and friend of Paul Howard.
"Tenderloin Vag" Bisbee Daily Review 29, May 1906 page 4

**Torres, Cyetana:** Deported to Mexico for being an immoral woman. Cyetana was using the name Guadalupe, but a distinctive scar clued immigration officers to her identity.
"Deportation Waits for Mexican Girl" Bisbee Daily Review 17, July 1909 page 5

**Trixy, Miss:** She was as arrested with a Miss Mattie for drunk and disorderly conduct behind the Annex Saloon. Trixy was fined $15.00 after pleading guilty.
"Ladies Arrested" Bisbee Daily Review 10, January 1903 page 8
"Paid $15" Bisbee Daily Review 11, January 1903 page 8

**Trout, Mrs. J.C.:** Worked in the red-light district before 1916.
"Details of Federal Prisoners' Escape from Jail Had" Bisbee Daily Review 9, June1916 page 5

**Tyson, Dora:** She operated No. 33 in 1909. Ms. Tyson was arrested along with Marie Happe, Hester Parker and Tempest Wyland in a red-light brawl that occurred on the night of May 5, 1911. She along with Marie Happe were fined $25. Dora was originally from Louisiana and was 28-years-old in 1910.

Connell, C. T. (1909, April, 20). Untitled letter [Letter to Commissioner General of Immigration]. Office of Inspector in Charge, Douglas, Arizona.
"Hate and Disorder in the Tenderloin" Bisbee Daily Review 7, May 1911 page 8
"Wholesale Arrests" Bisbee Daily Review 18, June 1912 page 6
U.S. Census Bureau (1910). Bisbee, Ward 1 Arizona Territory, Cochise County District 0005,

**Valdez, Consuela:** An ill-famed lady, who attacked Francisco Flores with a razor during a disagreement. Flores suffered a serious cut on the arm.

"Arizona Day by Day" The Arizona Republic 18, July 1899 page 3

**Vasquez, Josefa:** Arrested with Louisa Vasquez for operating a house out of the red-light district near the Calumet & Arizona Hospital in 1907. Josefa was sentenced to 60 days in jail.

"Untitled"" Bisbee Daily Review 23 August 1907 page 3

**Vasquez, Louisa:** She was arrested with Josefa Vasquez for operating a house out of the red-light district near the Calumet & Arizona Hospital in 1907. Both ladies were sentenced to 60 days in jail.

"Untitled"" Bisbee Daily Review 23, August 1907 page 3

French postcard c-1912

The Calumet & Arizona Hospital C-1907

**Vaughn, Gladys:** She is suspected of working in the red-light district in 1900.
U.S. Census Bureau (1900). Bisbee, Arizona Territory, Cochise County District 0007,

**Vella, Celia:** Was accused by Frank Schunk of stealing $30. She worked in the district in 1905,
"Says He was Robbed "Bisbee Daily Review 10, November 1905 page 8

**"Vera":** Worked in Bisbee in 1902 and was arrested for disturbing the peace. She was described in the Bisbee Daily Review as a *"rollick sage hen."*
"Brief City News" Bisbee Daily Review 14, October 1902 page 8

**"Vergie":** Attempted to commit suicide after being arrested by Officer Kempton.
"Officer Prevents Woman from Suicide" Bisbee Daily Review 26, February 1913 page 5

**Vickers, Hazel:** She was caring for May Davenport's jewelry while Davenport was in a sanitarium. It was stolen under her care.
"Jewelry Valued at $2,000 is Stolen" Bisbee Daily Review 8, May 1917page 2

**Voeltzel, Emma:** Operated the "Hog Ranch" in 1902. It was at her establishment that Ed Watts struck a miner named Andy Howard with a pick handle and knocked him down a flight of stone steps. She worked with Miss Davison, Miss Wilson and Miss Lupe.
"Howard Hit with Pick Handle" Bisbee Daily Review 3, June 1902 page 1
"Howard Back" Bisbee Daily Review 10, January 1903 page 8

**Waddell: Evelyn:** Arrested for vagrancy after being choked and hit by J.W. Skeels.
"Goes to Jail for Attacking Woman" Bisbee Daily Review 1, April 1917 page 8

**Walker, Belle:** In 1908, she was attacked by Nellie Burns with a knife.
"Negress Wields Knife" Bisbee Daily Review 20, October 1908 page 7

**Walsh, Hazel D:** It is believed, she worked in the district around 1907. She later left the red-light life and was married. Remarkably, Hazel was given at least some level of respectability and acceptance of her former profession. Parents and even the former Constable Bassett Watkins had no issue associating with her. Hazel died and was buried in Bisbee in 1969.
Richard Graeme III, Personal Communication February 12, 2017

**Watson, Lee:** An African-American madam who was stabbed by Rosie Highwarton, one of the girls working in her house. It was reported that Harry B. Highwarton held Lee as Rosie attacked her with a knife.
"Savage Attempt to Murder is Charged" Bisbee Daily Review 28, April 1907 page 5
"Bound Over to Await Action of Grand Jury" Bisbee Daily Review 1, May 1907 page 8

**Warden, Dolly:** This lady was 28 years old and recorded as being from Kentucky. She had lived in Bisbee about a year in 1916 and her parents were deceased.
Copper Queen Hospital Patients Register December 17, 1916 Bisbee Mining and Historical Museum, Bisbee.

**Williams, Mamie:** Abe Fields and J.W. Fanning, two who traveled along with carnivals stole $600.00 worth of jewelry from her. Her jewels included a, diamond ring, a large gold brooch with several diamonds, a pendant on a chain with three diamonds, large diamond earrings and a lady's watch with diamonds.
"Thieves Taken by Officers in Hot Pursuit" Bisbee Daily Review 26, March 1914 page 3
"$600 in Jewelry is Recovered; Stones Found in his Shoe" Bisbee Daily Review 27, March 1914 page 5

**Williams Nellie:** See Nora Desmon

**Williams Verna:** Attacked and seriously wounded May Burch with a knife.
"Assaulted her Companion with a Knife" Bisbee Daily Review 27, December 1908 page 8

**Wilmot, Mabel:** She was accused of stealing $150 while working in the red-light district
"Charges that Woman Stole Money" Bisbee Daily Review 1, October 1907 page 7

**Wilson, Lola:** Believed to have worked at No.41 in 1903. After Minnie Carey was found dying from morphine poisoning, Lola went to get a doctor and Minnie's daughter, Mabel Hastings.
"Cochise County Coroner's Inquest #114" Arizona State Archives Phoenix

**Wilson, Miss:** She was at the "Hog Ranch" when Ed Watts struck a miner named Andy Howard with a pick handle and knocked him down a flight of stone steps. She worked with Miss Davison, Emma Voeltzel and Miss Lupe.
"Howard Hit with Pick Handle" Bisbee Daily Review 3, June 1902 page 1
"Howard Back" Bisbee Daily Review 10, January 1903 page 8

**Wiston, Wilma:** This 26-year-old girl was from California and lived with Dora Tyson.
U.S. Census Bureau (1910). Bisbee, Ward 1 Arizona Territory, Cochise County District 0005,

**White, Bobby:** Assaulted by piano player Frank Haywood. Bobby was hospitalized on July 6, 1908 for alcoholism although, the newspaper implied it was from being beaten. The article also changes the name of the man who assaulted her from Frank Haywood to John Alden. Her mother was listed as Alline Burlage in Austin, Texas. Bobby had been in Bisbee two months and was 20 years-old.

"Beat up Woman did F. Haywood" Bisbee Daily Review 7, July 1908 page 5
"Jury Disagrees in Alden Case" Bisbee Daily Review 12, July 1908 page 5
Copper Queen Hospital Patients Register July 6, 1908 Bisbee Mining and Historical Museum, Bisbee.

**White Grace:** She was arrested for not having a license to operate an ill-famed house and operating a house out of the red-light district with Jessie Feilstan. Her bond was paid by Baptista Caretto. Note, that Caretto owned a building that was partly inside the district and the other section was outside the red-light district. This was after the district limits were increased from 1,200ft. from Central School to 1,300 ft. in 1906. Caretto had asked the city officials to place the structure entirely in the red-light district. Grace may have been working out of this building.

"Bawdy House Keepers" Bisbee Daily Review 26, January 1906 page 1

**Woodward, Marie:** In 1907, she was arrested for stealing money from a customer. She was keeping the change after selling him drinks.

"Short Changed Him" Bisbee Daily Review 15, March 1907 page 7

**Wortman, Cora:** See Cora Miles

**Wright, Nellie:** Operated No. 114 in 1909.

Connell, C. T. (1909, April, 20). Untitled letter [Letter to Commissioner General of Immigration]. Office of Inspector in Charge, Douglas, Arizona.

**Wyland, Tempest:** Ms. Wyland was arrested along with Marie Happe, Hester Parker and Dora Tyson in a red-light brawl that occurred on the night of May 5, 1911. Marie Happe filed a complaint and had her arrested.

"Hate and Disorder in the Tenderloin" Bisbee Daily Review 7, May 1911 page 8

**Zarillo, Rosa:** This girl was born in Bisbee. It is unknown whether she actually worked in Bisbee. She did work in an ill-famed house in Metcalf, Arizona and possibly El Paso, Texas.

Connell, C. T. (1909, June 14, 1909). No. 32A [Letter to Inspector in Charge, Tucson Office]. Office of Inspector in Charge, Douglas, Arizona.

**Zaslo, Birdie:** In 1901, she was 25 years-old and living with Marie Gusten in the red-light district. Originally, Birdie was from Washington.

U.S. Census Bureau (1910). Bisbee Ward 1, Arizona Territory, Cochise County District 0005

French postcard c-1910

A red-light district by a French artist   c-1910

# Vagrants, Miners, Customers, Lawmen, Fools, and other Ornery Characters

**Aguilar, Candelario:** was arrested with Dora Encinas for operating an ill-famed house out of the redlight district.
"Bisbee News" Tombstone Prospector 7, October 1899 page 3

**Aguirre, Fred:** This African-American was shot in the tenderloin.
"Personnel and Otherwise" Bisbee Daily Review 4, May 1904 page 6

**Alexander, Zac:** An African-American who witnessed the shooting of Glen Langford at the Canadian Club. Before the shooting he warned Langford to quiet down.
"Hall Released from Custody at Hearing" Bisbee Daily Review 22, September 1908 page 1

**Alden, Charles:** In 1908, Charles and John Hopkins were beaten up by two miners in the ill-famed district.
"Tenderloin Habitues Drubbed by Miners" Bisbee Daily Review 7, July 1908 page 5

**Ariola, Pedro:** Shot and killed Rosario Tapeta outside Anita Romero's House.
"Cochise County Coroner's Inquest #422" Arizona State Archives Phoenix

**Arroya, Ramon:** An employee of the Calumet & Arizona Mining company. He was arrested in 1908 for importing an immoral woman.
"Helped Bad Woman Enter Country "Bisbee Daily Review June 10, 1909 page5

**Atkinson, Charles:** He cashed a check with Emile Lefebvre. After the check was returned with *"No Funds"* written on it, Lefebvre had Atkinson arrested.
"Atkinson's Check Wasn't Valuable"" Bisbee Daily Review 1, February 1910 page 4

**Bailey L.R.:** Constable at Lowell 1909-1914. He testified against Felix Taylor at his trial. Also, he arrested B.J. Lacey and C.E. Beddinger for opium possession. Arthur McKerrarcher was apprehended by Bailey in the Neatherlin case.
"New Officials Start Today" Bisbee Daily Review 1, January 1909 page 5
"Takes Taylor "Harnessmaker gets it Tangle" Bisbee Daily Review 18, December 1909 page 8
Case Under Advisement." Bisbee Daily Review 2, May 1909 page 8
"Prisoners allege Warren has "Hop" Bisbee Daily Review 16, November1909 page 5

**Ball, George M.:** After, Glen Langford was shot at the Canadian Club, he picked up Langford's derringer and handed it to Ollie LePaige.
Hall Released from Custody at Hearing" Bisbee Daily Review 22, September 1908 page 1
"Ball Jury Disagreed" Bisbee Daily Review 24, September 1908 page 5
"Cases are Dismissed" Bisbee Daily Review 29, September 1908 page 7

**Bauer, Frank:** Deputy Sheriff 1907-1910. Testified at Frank Taylor's trial that he had seen Harriett Taylor being overly friendly with men at the Beer Garden.
"Takes Taylor Case Under Advisement." Bisbee Daily Review 2, May 1909 page8

**Bauer, Joe:** He was arrested for beating a woman in the restricted district.
"Serious Charge" Bisbee Daily Review 10, September 1908 page 7

139

**Bert, Frank:** In 1904, he was arrested for breaking down a door in the red-light district.
"On the Rampage "Bisbee Daily Review 5, January 1904 page 5

**Beddinger, C. E.:** Locally, known as *"Buck"* was arrested for smuggling opium from Naco, Sonora. Likely, the same person as C.E. Bittenger.
"Prisoners allege Warren has "Hop" Bisbee Daily Review 16, November 1909 page 5

**Bernardin, Alfredo:** During 1909, he was suspected of importing ill-famed girls into the U.S.
Connell, C. T. (1909, July 27). Untitled letter [Letter to commissioner General of Immigration]. Office of Inspector in Charge, Douglas, Arizona.

**Bishop, N.:** He accused Earnest Thomas of stealing money from him.
"Hearing this Afternoon" Bisbee Daily Review 14, April 1908 page 7

**Bittenger, C.E.:** Arrested for vagrancy in 1909. Likely, the same person as C.E. Beddinger
"Raid Nets Nine Undesirable Citizens"" Bisbee Daily Review 4, August 1909 page 1

**Black, Edward:** After drinking heavily, Black pulled a knife on red-light bartender Burt Connors. He was disarmed by someone and then Connors kicked him in the face.
"Two Slightly Hurt in Free-For-All" Bisbee Daily Review 12, January 1908 page 5
"Black Trial Today" Bisbee Evening Miner 16, January 1908 page 5

**Blackmore, (?):** A miner who was arrested for displaying a revolver while intoxicated in the district.
"Gun Toter Arrested" Bisbee Daily Review 19, April 1907 page 4

**Bohn, Adolph:** was seriously cut by soiled dove Inez Maritiana.
"Copperings" Tombstone Epitaph 20, August 1899 page 2

**Borders, W.D.:** In 1909, Borders was robbed in the district.
"Claims he was Robbed" Bisbee Daily Review 15, September 1909 page 6

**Bower, H.J.:** He was arrested for destroying a telephone in an ill-famed house.
"Bower fined $10" Bisbee Daily Review 23, December 1910 page 5

**Brayden, E.L.:** He was arrested at a house run by Louisa and Josefa Vasquez. The house was out of the restricted district and he was charged with vagrancy and given 60 days in jail.
"Untitled" Bisbee Daily Review 23, August 1907 page 3

**Breeding, S.B.:** During 1908, Breeding was arrested for fighting with J.V. Goggin.
"Held for Fighting" Bisbee Daily Review 12, March 1908 page 7

**Bringas, Jesus:** A witness to the shooting of Abundio Salas by Deputy Constable Francisco Jurado.
"Cochise County Coroner's Inquest #460" Arizona State Archives Phoenix

**Brooks, Walter:** Served as a city police officer from 1911-1914. Most of his arrests were for offenses, like hitching horses to fire hydrants or fighting in the red-light district. He was one of the officers that located an ill-famed house being operated behind Central school by May Gillis. After leaving the police force, he became a watchman for the Copper Queen Consolidated Mining Company. He was murdered by mescal smugglers while working as a watchman in 1915.
"Fast Driver Fined" Bisbee Daily Review 3, October 1911 page 4
"Raid House that is Near School" Bisbee Daily Review 23, April 1912 page 8
"Walter Brooks is Brutally Murdered When Attempt to Arrest is Made to Bootleggers" Bisbee Daily Review 29, June 1915 page 1
"Walter Brooks is Brutally Murdered" Bisbee Daily Review 29, June 1915 page 8

**Brown, Jack:** He was arrested stealing a stove. While examining him, the police discovered hypodermic needle marks on his arms and Brown was classified as a dope fiend.
"Attempts to Steal Stove; Caught in Act" Bisbee Daily Review 28, September 1919 page 2

**Brown, J.D.:** He was arrested by Deputy Sherriff Will White for carrying a Colt .45 revolver in the People's Theatre.
"Gun Toting Expensive" Bisbee Evening Miner 7, February 1907 page 1

**Brown, J.H.:** While he was in jail for living in a red-light house at Lowell, Arizona, he married the madam of the house, Annie Hooper. Ms. Hooper was 12 years the senior of the 23-year-old J.H. Brown. *"Frijoles"* a regular of the Bisbee jail gave away the bride.
"Versatile Frijoles Gave Away Bride" Bisbee Evening Miner 12, September 1907 page 5
"Wedding Services Performed in Jail" Bisbee Daily Review 12, September 1907 page 5

**Brown, Kid:** He came to Bisbee with Dot Foster, a 19-year-old girl that had supposedly belonged to an important San Francisco family. She had fallen into the lifestyle of the red-light. They were both arrested in Bisbee for stealing from an ill-famed house in Tucson.
"Well Connected" Bisbee Daily Review 23, May 1906 page 5

**Cardenas, Julian "Julius":** He operated the "Julian Cardenas Place" in the redlight district. It appears that he later leased the building to Emma Voeltzel and later sold it to her for $1,800.00. In 1901, Julian Cardenas shot and killed Jose Gonzales in front of the Turf Saloon on Main Street. Supposedly, Gonzales had paid too much attention to Cardenas' wife causing friction between them. According to the Tombstone Epitaph, Cardenas saw Jose Gonzales on the other side of the street and said, *"Don't you know you can't come to town." Gonzales responded with "Yes, I know it".* This was answer was answered with gun fire from Cardenas. Gonzales was killed. Julian Cardenas also operated the La Union Saloon on O.K. Street.

"Bisbee News" Tombstone Prospector 22, September 1897 page 3
"Advertisement" Arizona Daily Orb 1, August 1899 page 3
"Copperings" Tombstone Epitaph 20, August 1899 page 2
"County Records" Tombstone Epitaph 2, June 1901 page 4
"Bisbee Jottings" Tombstone Epitaph 3, November 1901 page 2
"Cochise County Coroner's Inquest #27" Arizona State Archives Phoenix
"County Recorder's Recent Work" Tombstone Epitaph 22, December 1901 page 4

**Caretto, Baptista (Baptiste):** A prominent citizen of Bisbee. He was a merchant and property owner Baptista and his wife witnessed the marriage of Mary Alice Bacon and Fredrick Fuss. The day after the marriage Mary was arrested for operating an ill-famed house out of district. In October of 1903, he broke up a knife fight between to drunken men at the O.K. Saloon. Baptista struck one man with a chair and seized his knife and the other man ceased fighting. Later, he was a member of jury that found Mrs. Thomas Fox guilty of practicing her profession outside the limits of the red-light district. In late 1905, Baptista offered to donate a $6,000 section of property to the city to build a school. This school would have forced the red-light district to move further up Brewery Gulch. The suggested school was not built, but the red-light district was moved 100 feet up the gulch after the completion of the new Central School building. This became problematic for Baptista as the new boundary left one of his buildings half in and half out of red-light district. Baptista asked for the city to consider the building as part of the red-light district, but the community declined. It is likely, that Grace White and Jessie Feilstan were arrested while working from this building.

"Marriage" Bisbee Daily Review 26, February 1903 page 5
"Lewd Women Arrested" Bisbee Daily Review 26, February 1903 page 4
"Mrs. Fuss is Acquitted" Bisbee Daily Review 27, February 1903 page 8
"Drew Knives in a Fight" Bisbee Daily Review 22, October 1903 page 8
"Mrs. Thos Fox is Found Guilty" Bisbee Daily Review 20, June 1905 page 5
"Bawdy House Keepers" Bisbee Daily Review 26, January 1906 page 1

**Carlise, J.L.:** He was arrested by Basset Watkins for vagrancy in the red-light district.

"Arrested on Reservation"" Bisbee Daily Review 4, August 1912 page 6

**Carron, Harry:** In 1913, he was arrested for vagrancy.

"No Room in City for These" Bisbee Daily Review 7, March 1913 page 3

**Casad R.A. "Bud":** Constable 1903-1904. In 1904, he was replaced by Biddy Doyle. During his tenure, he arrested Birdie Russell, Mrs. Mary A. Bacon, Grace Martin and Bell Hunter for operating an ill-famed house at the Opera Club. Later, he helped arrest Cora Miles for smoking opium and Mabel Carlise in the L.O. Milless murder case.

"Lewd Women Arrested" Bisbee Daily Review 26, February 1903 page 4
"Hop-Layout Found in House of Ill-Fame." Bisbee Daily Review 4, September 1903 page 1
"Sensation in James Case" Bisbee Daily Review 15, October 1903 page 4

**Cassady, D. Dr.:** A local eye doctor who forcibly entered the house of Fannie Roseman, while intoxicated. He refused to leave. After a time, Fannie was able to get him out, but then he proceeded to throw rocks through the windows. Finally, she fired two shots with a revolver to warn him away. Cassady's friend, Walter J. McCurdy was with him at the time. All were arrested, but the case was later dismissed. He worked in Bisbee from 1904-1908.

"Ugly Row in Tenderloin" Bisbee Daily Review 18, April 1908 page 5
"Cases Dismissed" Bisbee Daily Review 21, April 1908 page 7

**Casey, G.R.:** Locally, known as *"Rollin"* Casey, he shot Eugene Thompson after he tried to sit near him at the Happe Lunch Counter in the red-light district. The shooting occurred at 3:00 am in the ill-famed district.

"Shooting Scrape" Bisbee Daily Review 24, January 1909 page 7
"Preliminary Waived" Bisbee Daily Review 31, January 1909 page 7

**Cheney, J.M.:** He was arrested for assaulting and ill-famed girl in Brewery Gulch. His four gold teeth led to his identification and capture.

"Gold Teeth Prove to be his Undoing" Bisbee Daily Review 30, December 1911

**Chidester, George:** Deputy Sheriff in 1903-1904. He arrested Cora Miles and Joel Gibson for smoking opium. Later, he investigated the L.O. Milless murder case.

"Hop-Layout Found in House of Ill-Fame." Bisbee Daily Review 4, September 1903 page 1
"Officers Have Custody Men Supposed to have Killed L.O. Milles" Bisbee Daily Review 1, October 1903 page 1

**Clayton, Harry:** Arrested by Constable D.E. Twomey for assaulting an ill-famed lady.

"Vags Meeting Their Waterloo in Bisbee" Bisbee Daily Review 14, March 1908 page 5

**Coles, Charley:** In 1903, he smashed up the Cora Miles House.
"Raising a Rough House" Bisbee Daily Review 29, November 1903 page 5

**Coleman (?):** This man was arrested for carrying concealed weapon in the tenderloin district.
"Has a Gun Pay a Fine" Bisbee Daily Review 29, November 1903 page 5

**Connell, Charles T.:** Immigration inspector at Douglas, Arizona 1903-1910, after this he became immigration inspector for Tucson and later California. He investigated *"white slavery"* issues in Bisbee.
"Murphy Resigns as an Inspector" Bisbee Daily Review 26, February 1910 page 8
"Is Made Chief Inspector of Whole Service" Bisbee Daily Review 29, November 1910 page 1

**Conners, Bert:** He was reported as spending time in the red-light district in 1907. Later, he was noted as being a red-light bartender and Edward Black pulled a knife on him. After Black was disarmed, Connors proceeded to kick him in the face.
"Gun Packer is Given Stiff Fine" Bisbee Daily Review 11, April 1907 page 8
"Two Slightly Hurt in Free-For-All" Bisbee Daily Review 12, January 1908 page 5
"Black Trial Today" Bisbee Evening Miner 16, January 1908 page 5

**Cooper, Ike:** Locally, known as *"Ikie"* operated a house, but sold out in June of 1908.
"Ikie has Gone Had Many Troubles" Bisbee Daily Review 16, June 1908 page 8

**Cook, Pete:** He was arrested for vagrancy in 1909.
"Raid Nets Nine Undesirable Citizens'" Bisbee Daily Review 4, August 1909 page 1

**Contreras, August:** Operated a saloon and possible a house in the district in 1904. He was later indicted for kidnapping a girl from Aqua Prieta and putting her to work in Bisbee' red-light district. Madeline Armenta and Sabina Media were his accomplices.
"Warm Time in Tenderloin" Bisbee Daily Review 31, August 1904 page 1
"Federal Courts hold Boards at County Seat" Bisbee Daily Review 14, December 1904 page1
"Grand Jury will Finnish Today" Bisbee Daily Review 20, December 1904 page 1

**Craddock, Lee:** He was seen intoxicated in the red-light district. Later, he was arrested as a hold-up man.
"Stage Hold-up Men Nipped by Local Men" Bisbee Daily Review 19, April page 1

**Crow, J.F.:** In 1907, he was arrested for disturbing the peace in the district.
"Quintette of Disturbers" Bisbee Daily Review 11, April 1907 page 7

**Cummings, William:** Charged as being a *"lewd and dissolute person"* and accused of being a *"dope fiend"*. He was arrested in the red-light district.
"Cummings Chased out of the City" Bisbee Daily Review 15, January 1910 page 8

**Darkin, C. H. *"Red"*:** Arrested by Basset Watkins in the ill-famed district for vagrancy.
"Arrested on Reservation"" Bisbee Daily Review 4, August 1912 page 6

**Davis, C.:** He was arrested by Deputy Sherriff Chidester in an ill-famed house after holding up a man near the Shattuck Lumberyard.
"Bold Hold up near the Shattuck Lumberyard" Bisbee Daily Review 2, October 1903 page 1
"Thugs held to Answer" Bisbee Daily Review 7, October 1903 page 5

**Davis, J.M.:** He was arrested for fighting in the district along with Fay Greer, Hester Parker and Charles King.
"Tenderloin Fight" Bisbee Daily Review 27, April 1912 page 3

**DeeCoo, (?):** This gentleman ran up debts in the red-light district and then disappeared. He was described as well dressed and smooth talker.
"Another Genteel Gent with Gaft." Bisbee Daily Review 5, December 1903 page 8

**Douglas, W.D.:** Arrested by Constable D.E. Twomey for vagrancy in the red-light district.
"Officers Again After Vagrants" Bisbee Daily Review 4, March 1908 page 5

**Doyle, *"Biddy"* (Michael):** Constable from 1898 until the end of 1906. A witness to the shooting of Abundio Salas by Francisco Jurardo.
"New Officers Begin Work" Bisbee Daily Review 2, January 1907 page
"Cochise County Coroner's Inquest #460" Arizona State Archives Phoenix

**Doyle, D.D.:** He was beaten up when he choked a red-light girl.
"Looking for Trouble" Bisbee Daily Review 13, August 1904 page 5
"Cochise County Coroner's Inquest #460" Arizona State Archives Phoenix

**Dunbar, Thomas.:** Bartender at the Pike Saloon at Lowell, Arizona and husband of Dolly Dunbar, (Dolly Monbar) a madam of a house on Brewery Gulch. He had his jaw broken by John Miller one of his wife's customers.
"Dunbar's Jaw Broken by Rough" Bisbee Daily Review 9, August 1906 page 8

**Egan, J.W.:** This man arrested for vagrancy in 1909.
"Raid Nets Nine Undesirable Citizens"" Bisbee Daily Review 4, August 1909 page 1

**Erickson, John:** He was arrested for striking an ill-famed girl, Marie Eddie.
"Accused of Hitting Woman" Bisbee Daily Review 20, May 1908 page 7
"Six Cases Arise from Two Originals" Bisbee Daily Review 22, May 1908 page 5

**Easterman, F.H.:** Was fined $25 for fight in the tenderloin district.
"Fines Assessed" Bisbee Daily Review 1, June 1916 page 8

**Evans, Tom:** This African-American was sentenced to one year in a federal prison for possession of opium. He was arrested on Naco Road with his wife Fannie Evans, Will Martin and Edith Darnell. This may be the same Tom Evans who was wounded in a red-light brawl in Douglas, Arizona. As a bystander he was shot and wounded with a Springfield rifle.
"Negro Slain at Douglas" Bisbee Daily Review 12, June 1913 page 6
"Officers Raid Joint and Capture Opium Layout and Smokers" Bisbee Daily Review 19, October 1916 page 3
"Local Officers in Another Successful Raid on Opium Den" Bisbee Daily Review 20, 1916 page 8
"Sentenced to Prison" Bisbee Daily Review 22, November 1916 page 8

**Fagan, James:** Spent three days shooting up the tenderloin and was fined $75.00.
"Heavy Fine for Shooting "Bisbee Daily Review 6, November 1903 page 8

**Fanning, J.W.:** He was arrested with Abe Fields for stealing jewelry from red-light girl Mamie Williams. He tried to break out of jail twice.
"Thieves Taken by Officers in Hot Pursuit" Bisbee Daily Review 26, March 1914 page 3
"$600 in Jewelry is Recovered; Stones Found in his Shoe" Bisbee Daily Review 27, March 1914 page 5
"Jail Break is Foiled Two Times" Bisbee Daily Review 29, March 1914 page 1

**Farrel, Robert:** He helped operate the Casino in 1909.
Connell, C. T. (1909, April, 20). Untitled letter [Letter to Commissioner General of Immigration]. Office of Inspector in Charge, Douglas, Arizona.

**Finney, Arthur:** A one-legged gambler who stabbed Guillermo Romero in the abdomen in a disagreement over one of the girls that worked at Julius Cardinas Place. A few days later, Guillermo died and Finney was charged with murder. About this time, a women named Lucio (sp?) Romero tried to break Finney out of jail and was herself arrested.

On September 19, 1898, Finney was shot and killed by shot by John Slaughter. Arthur had hired a team of horses, a buggy and harness from the O.K. Livery Stable with the intent of traveling to La Morita. Instead, he indulged in mescal and sold the horses for 36 Mexican Dollars (silver 8-reale coins, possibly pesos) and then sold the buggy and harness for 96 more dollars. Later, he stole a six-shooter a Winchester rifle, a saddle and one of the horses he had sold. On the night of September 18, Justice Star Williams sent W.C. Smith to watch Finney's house on Chihuahua Hill and bring him in for selling the livery's property. At 9:00 am on the 19[th,] Smith reported that he had not found Finny.

Far to the Southeast, Deputy John H. Slaughter noticed Finney riding by his San Berdino Ranch (near what later would be Douglas, Arizona) about 7:00 am. He became was suspicious because the

Finney was obvious avoiding the house. A little while later, Finney met up with Rioz a ranch hand and engaged in a conversation to see if he could get a fresh horse from Rioz. Finney made it clear not to mention his presence to any "Americans." Lloyd L. Gilman a sheep rancher and witnessed Rioz and Finney talking. Meanwhile, John Slaughter called the custom house and learned he was wanted *"Dead or Alive"* by Justice Star Williams of Bisbee. A posse consisting of Lloyd L. Gilman, James H. Howard, Rioz, W.J. Chillis and Deputy John H. Slaughter found Arthur Finney asleep under a shade tree about 1 mile east of the San Bernadino ranch. The men surrounded Finney. Slaughter then approached the sleeping Finney and picked up his Winchester rifle and threw the rifle away from Finney and told him he was under arrest. Finney rose and pointed a cocked six-shooter at Slaughter's face. Quickly, with a 45-85 Marlin rifle, Slaughter fired reportedly removing three fingers and the pistols handle before striking him in the right breast. Gilman and Rioz also fired one bullet each and hit Finney's hip and the other hit his scalp.

Finney fell back dead and was buried nearby.

"Bisbee News" Tombstone Prospector 22, September 1897 page 3
"All Over Arizona" The Arizona Republic 28, September 1897 page 4
"Cochise County Coroner's Inquest #374" Arizona State Archives Phoenix
"Met the Wrong Man" The Weekley Orb 25, September 1898 page 3
"Bisbee Jottings" Tombstone Epitaph 25, September 1898 page 2

**Fields, Abe:** He robbed, red-light woman Mamie Williams and took $600.00 in jewelry that was later found in his shoe. A fine opium layout was seized from him during his arrest. Abe worked hard to escape the jail and actually dug through the brick wall with a fork and spoon. His escaped was foiled when he let a brick fall from the area he was digging and it almost hit a boy. This boy immediately went to the justice court and notified the officers. Later, that same day Abe was able to force open the door with a steel bar that he had smuggled in.

"Thieves Taken by Officers in Hot Pursuit" Bisbee Daily Review 26, March 1914 page 3

"$600 in Jewelry is Recovered; Stones Found in his Shoe" <u>Bisbee Daily Review</u> 27, March 1914 page 5
"Jail Break is Foiled Two Times" <u>Bisbee Daily Review</u> 29, March 1914 page 1

**Flores, Francisco:** was attacked by Consuela Valdez with a razor after becoming engaged in a dispute. Although, the woman tried to cut his throat, he raised his arm and was cut to the bone below the elbow. For a time, it was thought he was going to perish from blood loss, he recovered.
"Arizona Day by Day" <u>The Arizona Republic</u> 18, July 1899 page 3

**Frankel, Leo:** Arrested for disturbing the peace.
"Tenderloin Disturber" <u>Bisbee Daily Review</u> 23, September, 1909 page 6

***"Frijoles":*** Although, his real name was Salvadore Chacon (sp?), this man was normally called by his nickname *"Frijoles"* He seemingly felt he belonged in jail. On Saturday afternoons he would intentionally get arrested and would get free room and board until Monday. The newspaper reported, *"Frijoles enjoys the distinction of costing the county more money than any prisoner in the history of the county."* On one occasion Frijoles happened to be in jail when red-light lady Annie Hooper needed a man to give her away as a bride. She married J. H. Brown in the Bisbee jail with *"Frijoles"* giving her away.
"Versatile Frijoles Gave Away Bride" <u>Bisbee Evening Miner</u> 12, September 1907 page5
"Frijoles Paid Fine Whole Court Faints" <u>Bisbee Daily Review</u> 16, September 1909 page 2
"Frijoles has Returned to Old Haunts" <u>Bisbee Evening Miner</u> 3, September 1912 page3

**Gallagher, Harry:** In 1907, he was arrested for disturbing the peace in the district.
"Quintette of Disturbers" <u>Bisbee Daily Review</u> 11, April 1907 page 7

**Ghorin, Calvin:** He was arrested for being a habitué of the red-light district.
"Another "Vag" Case" <u>Bisbee Daily Review</u> 25, March1907 page 7

**Gibson, Joel:** He was arrested for smoking opium with Cora Miles.
"Hop-Layout Found in House of Ill-Fame." <u>Bisbee Daily Review</u> 4, September 1903 page 1
"Change of Venue in Tenderloin Case." <u>Bisbee Daily Review</u> 2, June 1906 page 6

**Gillan, Merill:** Likely, the same person as Merrill Gilland. He was charged with living off the gains of soiled doves.
"Undesirables Take French Leave" Bisbee Daily Review 25 July 1909 page 7

**Gilland, Merrill:** A piano player with a reputation of hanging out in the red-light district. Possibly the same person as Merrill, Gillan.
"Must Serve his Sentence" Bisbee Daily Review 6, October 1907 page 7

**Gillette, J.A.:** He was fighting with Charles Wilson at No.41. A revolver was fired and Constable White took the revolver from Gillette. It was suspected that Wilson had fired the pistol. Gillette was fined $10 and released.
"Mysterious Shot in Tenderloin" Bisbee Daily Review 14, April 1906 page 8

**Glover, A.:** Locally, known as *"Slivers"* and *"Slim"* was arrested for striking a red-light girl. Officer Frank Johnson heard rumors that Glover had said he planned to *"beat her head off" if she had not made any money."* Johnson proceeded to the district and arrested Glover after he witnessed him yelling at her.
"Tenderloin Habitue Beats Woman for Her Money" Bisbee Daily Review 18, July 1906 page 8

**Goggin, J.V.:** Arrested for fighting with S.B. Breeding.
"Held for Fighting" Bisbee Daily Review 12, March 1908 page 7

**Goforth, Isaac:** A witness to the shooting of Abundio Salas by Francisco Jurardo.
"Cochise County Coroner's Inquest #460" Arizona State Archives Phoenix

**Gortez, Ramon:** He was shot four times as he was walking to the red-light district. It is unclear whether the wounds were fatal.
"Mexican Shot This Morning Can't Recover." Bisbee Daily Review 10, July 1910 page 5

**Goudy, R.A.:** Witnessed the killing of William Phillips at the Little Casino.
"Cochise County Coroner's Inquest #263" Arizona State Archives Phoenix

**Graydon, A.:** In 1905, Graydon was arrested for vagrancy.
"In Justice Courts" <u>Bisbee Daily Review</u> 1, November 1905 page 5

**Green, H.L.:** He was arrested for fighting in the district, likely with Harry Lyons.
"Fast Driver Fined <u>Bisbee Daily Review</u> 3, October 1911 page 4

**Griffin, D.E.:** Charged with vagrancy.
"Vag's Must Seek Other Easy Places" <u>Bisbee Daily Review</u> 23, August 1907 page 5

**Hall, Henry:** The officer that arrested Helen Blanchard and Lena Frush in a tenderloin brawl. In September 1908, after resigning as an officer he became involved with the Beer Garden on Naco Road. On September 19, 1908, he shot and killed Glen Langford a gambler at the Canadian Club in the red-light district. During February 1909, Henry Hall again was placed on the police force. In 1911, he left Bisbee to work as a special officer for a mining Company at Ray, Arizona. He worked as an officer from 1908-1911.
"Woman is Fined Heavily for Fight." <u>Bisbee Daily Review</u> 28, October 1909 page 8
"Hall has Resigned Stevens on Duty" <u>Bisbee Daily Review</u> 2, September 1908 page 5
"Ex-policeman Henry Hall Shoots and Instantly Kills G. Langford" <u>Bisbee Daily Review</u> 19, September 1908 page 1
"Hall Gives Bond Langford Alive at Late Hour" <u>Bisbee Daily Review</u> 20 September 1908 page 9
"Hall Released from Custody at Hearing" <u>Bisbee Daily Review</u> 22, September 1908 page 1
"Temporarily James has Resigned" <u>Bisbee Daily Review</u> 11, February 1909 page 1
"Hall Leaves Today" <u>Bisbee Daily Review</u> 17, January 1912 page 8

**Hancock, William:** He was arrested for try to smuggle opium from Naco, Sonora to Bisbee.
"Hancock is Held on a "Hop" Charge" <u>Bisbee Daily Review</u> 14, April 1910 page 8

**Happe, Fred:** Involved in a tenderloin brawl.
"Hate and Disorder in the Tenderloin" <u>Bisbee Daily Review</u> 7, May 1911 page 8

**Happey, C.F.:** Struck John Erickson after he hit Marie Eddy.
"Six Cases Arise from Two Originals" <u>Bisbee Daily Review</u> 22, May 1908 page 5

**Hays, Ed:** Witnessed the shooting of Glen Langford at the Canadian Club.
"Hall Gives Bond Langford Alive at Late Hour" Bisbee Daily Review 20, September 1908 page 9

**Hayes, John P.:** This soldier was arrested for stealing two watches and $14 from a red-light girl. He was found in possession of the watches and a pocketbook. Hayes was turn over to the military for punishment. He was part of a regiment stationed at Naco.
"Soldier Arrested" Bisbee Daily Review 26, October 1916 page 3

**Haywood, Frank:** He was a piano player in the red-light district and was arrested for beating up a girl known as Bobby White.
"Beat up Woman did F. Haywood" Bisbee Daily Review 7, July 1908 page 5

**Henkel, Otto:** This red-light district piano player, was accused of stealing a saddle and bridle from ill-famed woman, Ada Beaumont.
"In Police Circles" Bisbee Daily Review 14, August 1906 page 3

**Henniger, George:** Worked the district likely, as a day shift piano player.
"Cochise County Coroner's Inquest #9" Arizona State Archives Phoenix

**Highwarton, Harry B.:** He reportedly held Madam, Lee Watson as Rosie Highwarton stabbed her with a knife.
"Savage Attempt to Murder is Charged" Bisbee Daily Review 28, April 1907 page 5
"Bound Over to Await Action of Grand Jury" Bisbee Daily Review 1, May 1907 page 8

**Hodge, A.J.:** Arrived at the Little Casino just after William Phillips was stabbed.
"Cochise County Coroner's Inquest #263" Arizona State Archives Phoenix

**Honeywell, R.L.:** Arrested for vagrancy in 1909.
"Raid Nets Nine Undesirable Citizens"" Bisbee Daily Review 4, August 1909 page 1

**Hoffmyer, Richard:** A witness to the morphine poisoning of Minnie Carey in No.41.
"Cochise County Coroner's Inquest #114" Arizona State Archives Phoenix

**Hopkins, John:** In 1908, John and Charles Alden were beaten up by two miners in the tenderloin district.

"Tenderloin Habitues Drubbed by Miners" Bisbee Daily Review 7, July 1908 page 5

**Howard, (Andrew) Andy:** He was at the "Hog Ranch" and entered an argument with Ed Watts. Reportedly, he climbed onto top of the bar and threatened to "cut the heart out of Ed Watts" Two of the girls drove him out of the ill-famed house with a chair. Then Ed Watts struck him with a pick handle and knocked him down a flight of twenty stone steps. Howard suffered a broken knee cap and injuries to the forehead that required stitches. Miss Davison, Miss Wilson, Emma Voeltzel and Miss Lupe, were the ladies involved. This is likely the same Andy Howard that had James Quinn arrested on grand larceny charges. Howard gave Quinn $50.00 to play poker, but James Quinn played faro instead. Quinn lost and Andy Howard had charges pressed against him. James Quinn was arrested at the Orient Saloon.

"Howard Hit with Pick Handle" Bisbee Daily Review 3, June 1902 page 1
"Howard Back" Bisbee Daily Review 10, January 1903 page 8
"Trial Today" Bisbee Daily Review 4, June 1902 page 8
"For Assaulting Howard" Bisbee Daily Review 5, June 1902 page 8
"Watts Bound over" Bisbee Daily Review 6, June 1902 page 8
"Two are Fined" Bisbee Daily Review 7, June 1902 page 8
"For Assaulting Howard" Bisbee Daily Review 5, December 1902 page 8
"Howard Back" Bisbee Daily Review 10, January 1903 page 8
"Howard Back" Bisbee Daily Review 10, January 1903 page 8
"Arrested for Losing" Bisbee Daily Review 21, October 1903 page 8

**Howard, Paul:** He was arrested for vagrancy in 1906.

"Tenderloin Vag" Bisbee Daily Review 29, May 1906 page 4

**Huskey, A.R.:** During 1909, Huskey was arrested for vagrancy.

"Husky Face Fails to be Seen in Court" Bisbee Daily Review 18, December 1909 page 4

**Hutchinson, Bob:** He was a prosecution witness that had seen Cora Miles and Joel Gibson smoking opium.

"Hop Joint Case is Dismissed" Bisbee Daily Review 5, September 1903 page 5

**James, Johnnie:** Charged with the murder of L.O. Milless. James was known to frequent the red-light district.
"Officers Have Custody Men Supposed to have Killed L.O. Milless" Bisbee Daily Review 1, October 1903 page 1

**James, Johnny:** Was appointed police officer in May 1908 to replace C.C. McCoy. He was accused of assaulting a man and resigned.
"Officer Appointed" Bisbee Daily Review 8, May 1908 page 7
"Officer James Arrested on Grave Charge Bisbee Daily Review 10, February 1909 page 1
Temporarily James has Resigned" Bisbee Daily Review 11, February 1909 page 1

**Jennings, Harry:** Constable 1902-1903. Helped arrest the murders of L.O. Milless, including their accomplice Mabel Carlise
Officers Have Custody Men Supposed to have Killed L.O. Milless" Bisbee Daily Review 1, October 1903 page 1
"New Police Officers" Bisbee Daily Review 14, February 1902 page 1
Officers Have Custody Men Supposed to have Killed L.O. Milles" Bisbee Daily Review 1, October 1903 page 1

**Johnson, Oscar:** After he was arrested, red-light girl, Virgil Bird tried to kill herself, but was saved by police officer Al Kempton.
"Officer Kempton was Life Saver" Bisbee Daily Review 5, December 1912 page 6

**Johnson, Victor:** He was arrested in 1913 for vagrancy.
"No Room in City for These" Bisbee Daily Review 7, March 1913 page 3

**Joiner, Lee:** Officer in 1909. He was the officer who arrested Leo Frankel. Joiner was later accused of deserting his wife and child.
"New Deputy Constable" Bisbee Daily Review 15, June 1909 page 5
"Tenderloin Disturber" Bisbee Daily Review 23, September, 1909 page 6
"Wife Charges She's Deserted" Bisbee Daily Review 6, October 1912 page 1

**Jones, Henry:** As a practical joke, he threw a stray dog into an ill-famed house. The unappreciative occupants of the house, beat him up.
"Trouble in Tenderloin Bisbee Daily Review 4, September 1904 page 3

**Jones, Thomas:** Arrested for vagrancy in 1913.
"No Room in City For These" Bisbee Daily Review 7, March 1913 page 5

155

**Jurado, Francisco:** Deputy Constable from about 1900-1901. He worked as deputy constable in the red-light district. In 1901, after he was no longer a constable he was killed when he resisting being arrested by Officer Johnson.
"Cochise County Coroner's Inquest #4" Arizona State Archives Phoenix
"Cochise County Coroner's Inquest #460" Arizona State Archives Phoenix

**Kempton, Al.:** Constable from 1912-1921 This officer was given credit for saving the life of ill-famed girl Virgil Bird. After he discovered she had drunk Lysol to kill herself, he immediately ran two and a half miles to fetch a doctor
"Allege Woman is a Vag" Bisbee Daily Review 26, October 1912 page 8
"Officer Kempton was Life Saver" Bisbee Daily Review 5, December 1912 page 6
Billy Brakefield named City Marshal" Bisbee Daily Review 6, July 1921page 7

**Kerner, Jake:** Operated No. 128 Brewery Gulch.
"Girl Plunges Knife Close to Miner's Heart" Bisbee Daily Review 14, October 1908 page5
"Bisbee Courts Grind out Grist" Bisbee Daily Review 8, September 1909 page 1

**King, Charles:** He was arrested for fighting in the district along with Fay Greer, Hester Parker and J.M. Davis.
"Tenderloin Fight" Bisbee Daily Review 27, April 1912 page 3

**Lacey, B.A.:** Arrested for vagrancy in 1909. Likely, the same person as B.J. Lacey.
"Raid Nets Nine Undesirable Citizens" Bisbee Daily Review 4, August 1909 page 1

**Lacey, B.J.:** Arrested for smuggling opium from Naco, Sonora. Possibly, the same person as B.A. Lacey.
"Prisoners allege Warren has "Hop" Bisbee Daily Review 16, November1909 page 5

**Langford, Glen:** This notorious gambler and card sharp was shot and killed by Henry Hall at the Canadian Club.
"Ex-policeman Henry Hall Shoots and Instantly Kills G. Langford" Bisbee Daily Review 19, September 1908 page 1

**Langford, Lou:** Arrested for vagrancy. He was well known as a gambler and possibly the same person as Glen Langford.

"Miner Sustained Broken Jaw Bisbee Daily Review 29, September, 1907 page 5
"Arrested for Vagrancy" Bisbee Daily Review 30, October, 1907 page 5

**Lawhorn, W.W.:** Indicted on charges of luring underage girls into immoral lifestyle with Kathryn Mabry.
"Girls Tell Story of Revolting Crime and Carousals" Bisbee Daily Review 10, December 1909 page 1
"Girls Tell Story of Revolting Crime" Bisbee Daily Review 10, December 1909 page 8
"Court Hears Mabry Case and Finds Woman Guilty" Bisbee Daily Review 14, December 1909 page 8
"Taken to Hospital" Bisbee Daily Review 15, January 1910 page 8

**Laybas, Ramon:** Accused of robbing rooms in the red-light district.
"Is Caught at Douglas" Bisbee Daily Review 11, February 1908 page 7

**Lefebvre, Emile: (Le Febere & Lefebvre)**
Operated the Canadian Club and suspected of being involved in the *"white slave"* traffic. He was describe as being tall, thin with graying hair and a black moustache. Generally, Emile was well dressed. In 1909, he was about 30 years old and had operated the Cozy Corner Saloon in Goldfield, Nevada. It was possibly an ill-famed house. Emile also went by the Alias Emile Lecomte. He continued to work in Bisbee until at least 1910.
Connell, C. T. (1909, June, 29). Untitled letter [Letter to Commissioner General of Immigration]. Office of Inspector in Charge, Douglas, Arizona.
Connell, C. T. (1909, July, 15). No. 32A [Letter to A. de la Torre]. Office of Inspector in Charge, Douglas, Arizona.
Copper Queen Hospital Patients Register July 4, 1909 Bisbee Mining and Historical Museum, Bisbee

**Leon, Rosendo:** was arrested for fighting with Anita Romero. He was expected to retain a significant scar from the brawl.
"Town Tattle" Arizona Daily Orb 19, July 1899 page 4

**LePaige, Ollie:** A piano player who likely worked at the Canadian Club. He was a witness to Glen Langford's shooting and was handed Langford's gun. Originally, he denied having the gun, but later turned over the two shot, .41 caliber derringer.
"Hall Gives Bond Langford Alive at Late Hour" Bisbee Daily Review 20, September 1908 page 9
"Hall Released from Custody at Hearing" Bisbee Daily Review 22, September 1908 page 1
"Ball Jury Disagreed" Bisbee Daily Review 24, September 1908 page 5
"Ollie Le Paige Trial Ends in Hung Jury" Bisbee Daily Review 25, September 1908 page 5

"Cases are Dismissed" Bisbee Daily Review 29, September page 7
"Atkinson's Check Wasn't Valuable"" Bisbee Daily Review 1, February 1910 page 4

**Lewis, Dell:** A former sheriff who reopened the Beer Garden in Johnson Addition in 1907 under the new name Riverside Park. This business had developed an unsavory reputation. Lewis appears to have tried to change this, but failed
"Officer Del Lewis Leases Beer Garden" Bisbee Daily Review 30, June 1908 page 5
"Riverside Park" Bisbee Daily Review 7, May 1909 page 7

**Lewis, J.K.:** He was arrested in the red-light district by Officer Henry Hall for being a *"lewd and dissolute person"*.
"Lewis Gets in Toils" Bisbee Daily Review 28, December 1907 page 7

**Lewis, Napoleon:** Jailed for morphine addiction.
"Is Dope Fiend" Bisbee Daily Review 17, February 1909 page 7
"A Dope Fiend" Bisbee Daily Review 19, February 1909 page 7

**Ligon, W.:** Arrested in 1912 for spending too much time in the red-light district.
"Police Court Case" Bisbee Daily Review 1, December 1912 page 5

**Luijada, Benino:** Stabbed William Philips at the Little Casino.
"Cochise County Coroner's Inquest #263" Arizona State Archives Phoenix

**Lyons, Harry:** Was arrested for fighting in the district, likely with H.L. Green
"Fast Driver Fined Bisbee Daily Review 3, October 1911 page 4

**Maddern, Charles:** He was at the house of Dolly Dunbar when her husband's jaw was broken by John Miller. He was struck by a chair swung by Fay Ellison during the brawl He was a bartender at the Reception Saloon.
"Dunbar's Jaw Broken by Rough" Bisbee Daily Review 9, August 1906 page 8
"Miller is Bound Over in Sum of $500"Bisbee Daily Review 11, August 1906 page 8

**Malen Walter:** In 1906, he was at the house of Dolly Dunbar when her husband's jaw was broken by John Miller.
"Dunbar's Jaw Broken by Rough" Bisbee Daily Review 9, August 1906 page

**Manor, Ray:** He was arrested for fighting in the red-light district.
"Wholesale Arrests" Bisbee Daily Review 18, June 1912 page 6

**Marshall, John:** In 1906, Marshall was arrested from stealing $200.00 from a miner named George Murphy. He proceeded to quickly spend the money in the red-light district before he was arrested.
"Man Charged with Robbery is Arrested" Bisbee Daily Review 9, November 1906 page 8

**Martin, Will:** Arrested for smuggling opium with Tom Evans, Fannie Evans and Edith Darnell.
"Officers Raid Joint and Capture Opium Layout and Smokers" Bisbee Daily Review 19, October 1916 page 3
"Local Officers in Another Successful Raid on Opium Den" Bisbee Daily Review 20, 1916 page 8

**Martz, Antonio:** This man accused a girl of stealing $115.00.
"Where is His $115?" Bisbee Daily Review 20, October 1907 page 7

**Maxwell, Pete:** He was arrested in the red-light district after cashing a forged check.
"Swindler taken by Swift Action" Bisbee Daily Review 9, December 1906 page 1

**McCoy, C.C.:** He was a police officer that was charged with disturbing the peace and having firearms and being drunk on duty. The complaint was filed by Margarete Gilliland a lady of the ill-famed profession. He was later found not guilty. McCoy served from August 1907-May 1908.
"Appointed to Police Force" Bisbee Daily Review 8, August 1907 page 7
"Officer McCoy Fined" Bisbee Daily Review 29, April 1908 page 7
"Charge against McCoy" Bisbee Daily Review 8, May 1908 page 7
"McCoy Not Guilty" Bisbee Daily Review 13, May 1908 page 7

**McCurdy, Walter J.:** He was attorney for Dr. Cassady and was with him in a rock throwing incident in the red-light district. McCurdy was not a Bisbee resident at the time.
"Ugly Row in Tenderloin" Bisbee Daily Review 18, April 1908 page 5
"Cases Dismissed" Bisbee Daily Review 21, April 1908 page 7

**McKerrarcher, Arthur:** Married Della Neatherlin a girl employed at No.41. Arthur was a saddle-maker by profession.
"Courtroom Looks Like House Party" Bisbee Daily Review 23, December 1909 page 3
"Harnessmaker gets it Tangle" Bisbee Daily Review 18, December 1909 page 8

**McRae, Parley:** A popular Bisbee constable from approximately 1909-1914. Although, he did make arrests in the ill-famed district, such as with the Lillie Neatherlin case and the battles between Dora Tyson and Marie Happe, His more interesting cases were dealing with *"The Woman in White"* a ghost that was bothering the families in Zacatecas Canyon. In another instance a goat who was chewing on a blanket was mistaken for a body in the last moments of death.
"Courtroom Looks Like House Party" Bisbee Daily Review 2, December 1909 page 3
"Ghostly Visitations Disturbing Zacatecas" Bisbee Daily Review 17, October 1909 page 8
"Officers Find Goat Chewing up Blanket" Bisbee Daily Review 8, December 1909 page 5
"Hate and Disorder in the Tenderloin" Bisbee Daily Review 7, May 1911 page 8

**Miller, Harry:** Operated the Canadian Club at the time Glen Langford was shot and killed by Henry Hall.
"Hall Gives Bond Langford Alive at Late Hour" Bisbee Daily Review 20, September page 9

**Miller, Jake:** A witness to a fight between Lena Frush and Millie Brown.
"Bisbee Courts Grind out Grist" Bisbee Daily Review 8, September 1909 page 1

**Miller, Harry:** He was accused of white slavery for paying the railroad fare of an ill-famed lady to Bisbee.
"Miller's Bondsmen Will Have to Pay up" Bisbee Daily Review 23, December 1911 page 6

**Miller, John:** A miner who began to fight with Thomas Dunbar, the husband of Dolly Dunbar a madam on the gulch. He supposedly broke

Thomas' jaw with a rock. Charles Maddern, William Robertson and Ed Shearer were at the Ill-famed house at the time.
"Dunbar's Jaw Broken by Rough" Bisbee Daily Review 9, August 1906 page 8
"Miller is Bound Over in Sum of $500" Bisbee Daily Review 11, August 1906 page 8

**Miller, J.A.:** He witnessed to the stabbing of William Phillips at the Little Casino.
"Cochise County Coroner's Inquest #263" Arizona State Archives Phoenix

**Moore, Teddy:** A piano player that worked at Mrs. Geary's in the ill-famed district. He cared for the injured Oscar Young. "Cochise County Coroner's Inquest #9" Arizona State Archives Phoenix

**Mosely, Frank:** A miner who stole a diamond brooch from Irene Brown and buried it in his yard. The brooch was returned.
"Valuable Jewel is Returned Through Effort of Officers" Bisbee Daily Review 10, August 1915 page 8

**Muffitt, James Vick:** He was accused of grand larceny of the Copper Queen Store and was known to spend time in the district. Muffitt had the reputation of giving the ladies expensive champagne and other items. He left Bisbee in 1903.
"Reward Offered for J.V. Muffitt" Bisbee Daily Review 6, January 1903 page 4

**Murphy, Owen E.:** Justice of the Peace 1905-1906. He was noted for scolding two 17-year boys that had been arrested drinking in the red-light district. He recommended they give their money to their parents rather than drink. The boys were released with a firm warning.
"Lads in Justice Court" Bisbee Daily Review 27, December 1905 page 5

**Murphy, "Spud":** In 1907, he was arrested for vagrancy.
"Arrested for Vagrancy" Bisbee Daily Review 30, October, 1907 page 5

**Murphy, T.A.:** He wrote a bad check in the district and was arrested.
"Alleged Bad Check" Bisbee Daily Review 4, March 1908, page 7

**Nass, Jacob:** During 1908, he was arrested by Constable D.E. Twomey for vagrancy in the red-light district

"Officers Again After Vagrants" Bisbee Daily Review 4, March 1908 page 5

**Nelson, Frank:** He admitted to kissing Harriet Taylor, the wife of Felix Taylor in his trial. He also stated that he felt the Beer Garden was not the place for a decent woman.
"Two Prisoners will be Arraigned Today." Bisbee Daily Review 1, May 1909 page5
"Takes Taylor Case Under Advisement." Bisbee Daily Review 2, May 1909 page8

**Noftz, Bert:** This man frequented the red-light district. Later, he was convicted of murdering L.O. Milless a roulette dealer at the Brewery Saloon.
"Officers Have Custody Men Supposed to have Killed L.O. Milles" Bisbee Daily Review 1, October 1903 page 1

**Nolan, Martin:** He saw the flash of the knife as William Phillips was fatally stabbed at the Little Casino.
"Cochise County Coroner's Inquest #263" Arizona State Archives Phoenix

**Oldham, Bruce:** During 1908, he was arrested for vagrancy in the red-light district.
"Raid Nets Nine Undesirable Citizens"" Bisbee Daily Review 4, August 1909 page 1

**Oliver, Joe:** He shot and seriously wounded, C.H. Smith, the husband of Mae Scott. Oliver escaped from the county jail and disappeared.
"Shooting Scrape Cost One Liberty and Other His Arm" Bisbee Daily Review 22, February 1914 page 1
"Two Break Jail Early in Morning" Bisbee Daily Review 22, February 1914 page 1
"2 Captured in Naco" Bisbee Daily Review 24, February 1914 page 3
"2 Captured in Naco; Hunt Continues" Bisbee Daily Review 24, February 1914 page 1

**O' Connor, Clare:** In 1907, he was arrested for disturbing the peace in the district.
"Quintette of Disturbers" Bisbee Daily Review 11, April 1907 page 7

**Ovens, Ray:** After fighting with a district girl, he was fined $7.00.
"Officers seek Alleged Offenders." Bisbee Daily Review 19, November 1905 page 5

**Owen, R.O.:** This man was arrested for disturbing the peace at Dolly Dunbar's House. He was a salesman and tried to procure business from the house for M & O Cleaners.
"Owens's Case Dismissed" Bisbee Daily Review 14, November 1909 page 5

**Parker, Shelby:** He was arrested for vagrancy with Ethel Sheriff and was accused of using opium.
"City Police Arrest Parker" Bisbee Daily Review 30, September 1902 page 8

**Parham, Gordon:** Charles B. Young was slashed by Parham with a knife at the Little Casino in an upstairs room.
"Cutting Affray in Redlight District" Bisbee Daily Review 13, March 1909 page 1
"Young has Good Chance to Recover" Bisbee Daily Review 14, March 1909 page 8

**Parks, L.:** While carrying a gun in the district, he was arrested. His name was believed to be an alias and not his true name.
"Gun Packers are Shown Little Mercy" Bisbee Daily Review 16, May 1907 page 8

**Pennington, W.H.:** He was arrested for vagrancy, but oddly, it was a woman of the red-light district that filed the complaint. This was the first time an ill-famed woman had filled such a complaint. It is possible that this charge resulted from him being involved with a brawl in the red-light district between Dora Tyson and Marie Happe
"Hate and Disorder in the Tenderloin" Bisbee Daily Review 7, May 1911 page 8
"Given Stiff Fines" Bisbee Daily Review 10, May 1911 page 2

**Phillips A. J.:** The brother of William Phillips, he witnessed the fatal stabbing of his William at the Little Casino.
"Cochise County Coroner's Inquest #263" Arizona State Archives Phoenix

**Phillips, William:** At only 17-years-old, he was stabbed to death at the Little Casino by Benino Luijada.
"Cochise County Coroner's Inquest #263" Arizona State Archives Phoenix

**Printy, J. Ed.:** Owner of the Little Casino Saloon in the red-light district. During this time, he became entangle in a brawl with Deputy

Sheriff John M. Johnson. Printy preceded to nearly beat the officer to death after he pulled a gun on him. Problems continued on September 7, 1904. In Douglas, at the Queen Hotel Bar, Printy drew a gun on Johnson and a fight began. Printy was better known for holding bronco busting contests.

"Saloon Man Mauls Officer" Bisbee Daily Review 18, August 1904 page 1
"Printy Act May be Fatal Bisbee Daily Review 19, August 1904 page 1
"Printy Opens Gun Feud at Douglas "Bisbee Daily Review 7, September 1904 page 1
"The Case as it Stands "Bisbee Daily Review 8, September 1904 page 1
"Ad" Bisbee Daily Review 22, December 1905 page 3

**Rae, James:** He was fined $25 for fighting in the district.

"Fines Assessed" Bisbee Daily Review 1, June 1916 page 8

**Randolph, Charles:** This man was found guilty of vagrancy in Lowell, Arizona. He was arrested with a girl with the surname Reed. This girl had worked the red-light district on the gulch.

"Undesirables are Given Jail Terms" Bisbee Daily Review 12, November 1910 page 8

**Reardon, George:** Dolly Dunbar attacked him with a straight razor.

"Tries to Cut Throat of Guest" Bisbee Daily Review 6, June 1911 page 8
"Dunbar Case Before High Judge." Bisbee Daily Review 15, June 1911 page 5

**Retabone, Beet:** He was arrested for disturbing the peace in the district.

"Quintette of Disturbers" Bisbee Daily Review 11, April 1907 page 7

**Riaz, Antonio:** Mabel Wilmot was accused of stealing $115.00 from Antonio.

"Charges That Woman Stole Money" Bisbee Daily Review 15, October 1907 page 7

**Ritner, Victor:** A miner who was arrested with May Gillis for operating an ill-famed house near Central School. In 1920 he married Ms. Gillis.

"Raid House that is Near School" Bisbee Daily Review 23, April 1912 page 8

**Ritz, Charles:** He was arrested for smoking opium in the ill-famed district, during 1902.

"Opium Den Raided" Bisbee Daily Review 26, January 1902 page 4

**Robertson, R. William:** A miner, who was at the Dunbar house the night, John Miller broke Thomas Dunbar's jaw.
Dunbar's Jaw Broken by Rough" Bisbee Daily Review 9, August 1906 page 8
"Miller is Bound Over in Sum of $500" Bisbee Daily Review 11, August 1906 page 8

**Robinson, Eugene:** He was arrested for vagrancy.
"Crusade is on in the Tenderloin "Bisbee Daily Review 31, July 1908 page 8

**Robinson, Otis:** This man was arrested on a warrant from Douglas, Arizona in Bisbee's red-light district.
"Two Arrests Made in Bisbee Tenderloin" Bisbee Daily Review 22, October 1909 page 8

**Roe, Richard:** A miner for Wolverine & Arizona Mining Company. He was wrongly arrested for vagrancy.
"Cold Chills for the Tenderloin" Bisbee Daily Review 21, October 1905 page 5

**Rosenwald, Abraham A.:** He was describe as being 5' 5" tall heavy set with dark eyes and about 25 years old. Also, Rosenwald was supposed to have worked with Jewish ill-famed ladies in El Paso, Texas before moving to Bisbee. Rosenwald was arrested for vagrancy in 1909 and left Bisbee with Sadie Kline and Ida Rosenwald.
Connell, C. T. (1909, June 14, 1909). No. 32A [Letter to Thos. M. Fisher jr.]. Office of Inspector in Charge, Douglas, Arizona.
"Rosenwald Fails to Appear for Trial" Bisbee Daily Review 5, June 1909 page 5

**Ruff, Hill G.:** Officer from 1908- around 1920. He made a number of arrests dealing with illegal alcohol. Ruff is best remembered for an important cocaine and morphine bust he helped make on Naco Road in 1916.
"Several "Dope" Venders are Arrested in the City" Bisbee Daily Review 27, April 1916 page 1

**Sada, Lewis:** He was arrested for fighting the district with Helen Brown. She fired shots at him.
"Row in Tenderloin "Bisbee Daily Review 17, May 1908 page 7
"Six Cases Arise from Two Originals" Bisbee Daily Review 22, May 1908 page 5

**Salas, Abundio:** This man was shot and killed by Deputy Constable Francisco Jurado in the district, during 1901.
"Cochise County Coroner's Inquest #460" Arizona State Archives Phoenix

**Salazar, A.S.:** Witnessed the killing of William Philips at the Little Casino.
"Cochise County Coroner's Inquest #263" Arizona State Archives Phoenix

**Schunk, Frank:** Celia Vella was accused of stealing $30 from him. She said he spent it all on drinks.
"Says He was Robbed "Bisbee Daily Review 10, November 1905 page 8

**Shea, Cornelius (Con):** He and his wife Lillian Shea operated a house on Brewery Gulch and later, one in Lowell. Con originally came from Jerome and possibly, died there in 1913.
"Con Shay is Found Guilty" Bisbee Daily Review 2, March 1904 page 5

**Shearer, Ed.:** A painter for Stonehouse Signs, He was at the Dunbar house on the night John Miller broke Thomas Dunbar's jaw.
"Dunbar's Jaw Broken by Rough" Bisbee Daily Review 9, August 1906 page 8
"Miller is Bound Over in Sum of $500" Bisbee Daily Review 11, August 1906 page 8

**Sheridan, C.P.:** He was arrested for passing a fake gold nugget that he had made from copper and brass.
"Passes Copper for Gold Nugget" Bisbee Daily Review 4, March 1906 page 8

**Skeels, J.W.:** After hitting and choking Evelyn Waddell, he was arrested.
"Goes to Jail for Attacking Woman" Bisbee Daily Review 1, April 1917 page 8

**Smith, C.H.:** Local miner and husband of Mae Scott who was shot and wounded by Joe Oliver.
"Shooting Scrape Cost One Liberty and Other His Arm" Bisbee Daily Review 22, February 1914 page 1
"Two Break Jail Early in Morning" Bisbee Daily Review 22, February 1914 page 1
"2 Captured in Naco" Bisbee Daily Review 24, February 1914 page 3
"2 Captured in Naco; Hunt Continues" Bisbee Daily Review 24, February 1914 page 1

**Smith *"Cokehead"*:** He was an accused drug addict who was forced to leave Bisbee.
"Business is Brisk on Police Blotter" Bisbee Daily Review 18, September 1919 page 8

**Smith, Harry:** Had a wife in the district in 1910.
"Officer Loses his Prisoner on way North Bisbee Daily Review 2, February 1910 page 5

**Smith, J.W.:** A miner from Germany who was brutally stabbed by Ruby Davis in front of No. 128 Brewery Gulch. He remained in the Copper Queen Hospital 15 days.
"Girl Plunges Knife Close to Miner's Heart" Bisbee Daily Review 14, October 1908 page 5

**Smith, Frank, Lieutenant:** This officer was in charge of the U.S. Army Provost Guards and removed soldiers from the district belonging to units stationed at Naco, Arizona.
"Provost Guard Troubles" Bisbee Daily Review 2, December 1916 page 8

**Snodgrass, Hank:** City Marshall 1904-1908. He was involved in the investigation of the murder of Henry Savage by Kate Savage a former red-light madam.
"Alleged Murders Taken to Tombstone" Bisbee Daily Review 11, August 1905 page 5

**Snow, Harry:** He operated a restaurant in the red-light district.
"Jury Says Not Guilty" Bisbee Daily Review 19, November page 5

**Stevens, George:** This man was accused by and later cleared of stealing $7.00 in from an ill-famed girl.
"Is Cleared by Jury" Bisbee Daily Review 15, August 1907 page 7

**Stevens, Jack:** A city marshal. He forwarded a campaign to rid the red-light district of vagrants living off the less than virtuous women.
"Rock pile for Buzzards of Redlight" Bisbee Daily Review 11, October 1908 page 5

**Stolwell, R.H.:** He worked as a moving picture promoter and was arrested on vagrancy.
"Hogan puts a $50 Fine on Stolwell" Bisbee Daily Review 17, April 1910 page 5

**Stone, A.F.:** An unscrupulous character who stole the money raised to pay for red-light girl, Rubie Raymond's medical expenses. She was suffering from typhoid.
<sub></sub>"Stole Money Given to Unfortunate Woman"" <u>Bisbee Daily Review</u> 4, June 1907 page 5
"May Reduce Charge Against Defendant"" <u>Bisbee Daily Review</u> 9, June 1907 page 5
"Pleads Guilty to Charge"" <u>Bisbee Daily Review</u> 13, June 1907 page 7

**Tapeta, Rosario:** Shot and killed by Pedro Ariola near Anita Romero's House.
"Cochise County Coroner's Inquest #42" Arizona State Archives Phoenix

**Taylor, Felix:** Arrested for prostituting his wife, sister and mother in Lowell. His later prosecution focused on his actions with his wife Harriet Taylor.
"Two Prisoners will be Arraigned Today." <u>Bisbee Daily Review</u> 1, May 1909 page 5
"Takes Taylor Case Under Advisement." <u>Bisbee Daily Review</u> 2, May 1909 page 8

**Telley, Albert:** An insurance salesman who was reported to have wanted to marry Lily Silver in order to prevent her from being deported back to France. Later, he told the newspaper that his statements were not serious.
"Would Marry French Girl to Save Her" <u>Bisbee Daily Review</u> 12, July 1908 page 5
"No Wedding Bells or Me Says Telley" <u>Bisbee Daily Review</u> 14, July 1908 page 1

**Thomas, Earnest:** He was accused of stealing money from N. Bishop.
"Hearing this Afternoon" <u>Bisbee Daily Review</u> 14, April 1908 page 7

**Thompson, Dan:** During Arizona's prohibition, this man became entangled with the law after he had sold three ill-famed ladies beer. This was supposed to have occurred on two separate occasions and from his house on Tombstone Canyon. His wife's charges were suspended and he paid $100 fine.
"Thompsons' Found Guilty to appeal Decision of Court." <u>Bisbee Daily Review</u> 9, May 1917 page 5

**Thompson, Eugene:** An African-American who was shot by G.R. Casey at the Happe Lunch Room.
"Shooting Scrape" Bisbee Daily Review 24, January 1909 page7
"Preliminary Waived" Bisbee Daily Review 31, January 1909 page7

**Tisdale, John:** Locally, known as the *"Overall Kid"* was arrested for vagrancy.
"Vagrant Nabbed" Bisbee Daily Review 24, June 1906 page 5

**Tomas, Jose:** was arrested for stealing bottles of beer from the "Mexican Dance Hall".
"Copperings" Tombstone Epitaph 3, September 1899 page 2

**Turner, Jake:** A janitor/ porter that worked in red-light district, likely at Anita Romero's Place.
"Cochise County Coroner's Inquest #9" Arizona State Archives Phoenix

**Twomey, D. E.:** He became a Bisbee constable on January 2, 1907 and worked until 1911. Twomey arrested two men named Newton and Garland for smoking opium in the red-light district and was one of the officers who investigate Glen Langford's shooting.
"New Officers Begin Work" Bisbee Daily Review 2, January 1907 page 2
"Officers Surprise Two Opium Fiends" Bisbee Daily Review 29, May 1907 page 5
"Ex-policeman Henry Hall Shoots and Instantly Kills G. Langford" Bisbee Daily Review 19, September 1908 page

**Tyson, William:** He operated an ill-famed house in 1910.
U.S. Census Bureau (1910). Bisbee, Ward 1 Arizona Territory, Cochise County District 0005,

**Verleye, R.S.:** A man who was arrested for forging checks and was known to visit the red-light district.
"Arrested on a Charge of Forgery" Bisbee Daily Review 16, September 1906 page 8

**Wade, Clark:** This man was arrested for spending too much time in the red-light district. He had steady employment and was released on a promise of good behavior.
"Found Guilty" Bisbee Daily Review 7, June 1917 page 6

**Walsh, Bert:** A piano player, likely at the Canadian Club where he witnessed the shooting of Glen Langford.
"Hall Released from Custody at Hearing" Bisbee Daily Review 22, September 1908 page 1

**Warren, George:** He was arrested in the Ozark Rooming House with Dollie St Clair for possession of opium.
"Local; Officers in Another Successful Raid on Opium Den" Bisbee Daily Review 20, October 1916 page 8

**Wasserman, Morris:** This man paid a $10 fine for fighting in the red-light district. Dora Tyson, Marie Happe and Ray Manor were also charged. In 1913, he operated the Canadian Club and was arrested for allowing gambling.
"Wholesale Arrests" Bisbee Daily Review 18, June 1912 page 6
"Bad Luck in Bunches is His" Bisbee Daily Review 1, October 1913 page 5

**Waters, Robert:** He was arrested for disturbing the peace in the district.
"Quintette of Disturbers" Bisbee Daily Review 11, April 1907 page 7

**Watkins, Bassett:** Constable from 1910-1914. He recovered the stolen jewelry of "Roxie" a red-light girl. Also, Bassett helped locate the ill-famed house run by May Gillis near Central School. Later he worked as a miner.
"Missing Jewels Returned" Bisbee Daily Review 25, September 1910 page 5
"Raid House that is Near School" Bisbee Daily Review 23, April 1912 page 8

**Watson, F.W.:** In 1908, he was arrested for vagrancy.
"Watson is Vagged" Bisbee Daily Review 26, July 1908 page 7

**Watson, Jack:** Officer Brooks arrested him at the Majestic for vagrancy.
"Vagrant Accessed Fine of 50 Plunks"" Bisbee Daily Review 22, April 1912 page 5

**Watts, Ed:** He became engaged in an argument with a miner named Andy (Andrew) Howard at the Hog Ranch. According to the newspaper, Howard was drunk and climbed on the bar and was holding a knife. He told Watts that he was going to "cut Watts' heart out" One of the ladies drove Howard out a door with a chair and Ed struck him with a pick handle. Howard was knocked down twenty stone steps and broke a knee. Ed Watts turned himself in to law enforcement and was found not guilty at his trial. The only witness refused to testify. Miss Davison Miss Wilson, Emma Voeltzel and Miss Lupe were the red-light girls present. The girls were arrested for helping during the fight. Two of the girls were fined $10.00 and the other two were released due to lack of evidence.

"Howard Hit with Pick Handle" Bisbee Daily Review 3, June 1902 page 1
"Trial Today" Bisbee Daily Review 4, June 1902 page 8
"For Assaulting Howard" Bisbee Daily Review 5, June 1902 page 8
"Watts Bound over" Bisbee Daily Review 6, June 1902 page 8
"Two are Fined" Bisbee Daily Review 7, June 1902 page 8
"For Assaulting Howard" Bisbee Daily Review 5, December 1902 page 8
"Howard Back" Bisbee Daily Review 10, January 1903 page 8

**Welch, Burt:** During 1906, he was arrested for assaulting Trixy Fawcett. Later he was arrested for vagrancy.
"Bawdy House Row" Bisbee Daily Review 11, July 1906 page 5
"Raid Nets Nine Undesirable Citizens"" Bisbee Daily Review 4, August 1909 page 1

**Welsh, James:** This man was arrested for being drunk and disorderly in the red-light district. Later, he accused Jennie Joe of pointing a revolver at him.
"Rough House in Red Light on Trial Today" Bisbee Evening Miner 4, September 1907 page 1

**White, (?):** The star pitcher of the Bisbee Ball Club. In 1902, he was stabbed by "Black Fanny" at no.10 in the red-light district.
"Ball Player is Stabbed" Bisbee Daily Review 21, August 1902 page 5

**White, Jack:** Bisbee Constable in 1905. He went to Douglas, Arizona to arrest Katie Mattison. Katie had assaulted another girl in a red-light house located in Brewery Gulch and had fled to Douglas. In April of 1905, Constable White prevented S. Uralez from stabbing Amy Harris with a knife. Amy was and African-American resident of Brewery Gulch and had been living with Uralez. It is not clear whether Ms.

Harris was and ill-famed lady. In 1906, he arrested, soiled-dove May Norton for stealing $125. Constables, Wilmoth and White later raided the Norton House which was suspected to be operating as a house of ill-repute, outside the designated district. Later in 1906, he arrested, soiled-dove, Dot Foster on a warrant from Tucson. He became a sheriff in 1907.

"Brought Woman Back" Bisbee Daily Review 15, February 1905 page 6
"Mexican Probably Prevented from Murder" Bisbee Daily Review 27, April 1905 page 5
"Woman is Arrested for Robbery of Man" Bisbee Daily Review 8, April 1906 page 1
"House is Raided" Bisbee Daily Review 11, April 1906 page 8
"Well Connected" Bisbee Daily Review 23, May 1906 page 5
"New Officers Begin Work" Bisbee Daily Review 2, January 1907 page 2

**White, William (Bill) (Will):** Deputy Sheriff and brother to Sheriff Jack White. Soon after becoming deputy, he helped arrest, Bautista Marinoni a man who killed two miners on Brewery Gulch. The murder occurred in a lumberyard just below the red-light district, he disappears from Bisbee's history in 1911. He was deputy from 1907-1911.

"Marinoni Case Wil be Called Monday" Bisbee Daily Review 11, May 1911 page 8

**Whitfield, Charles:** He was arrested by Constable Biddy Doyle for interfering with the arrests of Bessie Hight and Mary Moore.

"Trouble at the Beer Garden" Bisbee Daily Review 16, July 1902 page 1

**Williams, John S.:** A district attorney that fought to prevent the City of Bisbee from licensing the red-light houses. This was an effort to eliminate the ill-famed women from Bisbee.

"Bisbee Council Throws City Wide Open" Bisbee Daily Review 23, October 1909 page 1

**Williams Starr K.:** Justice of Peace and Coroner (S.K. Williams) 1897-1903 and attorney until after 1922. During his term as Justice of the Peace, he was found guilty of gambling at roulette. Later, he was the defense attorney for former madam Mildred Savage. Also, he defended Felix Taylor who was accused of prostituting his own wife.

"Complete Report of the Grand Jury" Bisbee Daily Review 18, December 1901 page 1

"Mrs. Savage in Jail" Bisbee Daily Review 5, August 1905 page 1
"Takes Taylor Case Under Advisement." Bisbee Daily Review 2, May 1909 page 8

**Wilson, (?):** A bartender in the red-light district in 1904.
"Was Not Guilty" Bisbee Daily Review 7, July 1904 page 5

**Wilson, Charles:** In 1906, he became engaged in a fight with J.A. Gillette in No.41. During the quarrel, he became seriously beaten around the head. It is believed Charles fired a pistol, but no one was injured. Gillette took the revolver from Wilson in the fight. They were both arrested and Charles was fined $50.
"Mysterious Shot in Tenderloin" Bisbee Daily Review 14, April 1906 page 8

**Wilmoth, Jay F.:** A law enforcement officer from 1904 to at least 1922. He discovered the Norton House was actually operating as an out of red-light district, ill-famed house. Wilmoth also, was involved in the Lewis Sada and Helen Brown brawl. During the shooting at the Bisbee Daily Review office in 1909 Wilmoth was wounded in the right arm.
"New Night Officer" Bisbee Daily Review 8, April 1904 page 5
"House is Raided" Bisbee Daily Review 1, April 1906 page 8
"Six Cases Arise from Two Originals" Bisbee Daily Review 22, May 1908 page 5
"Double Tragedy in Review Office Stirs Bisbee" Bisbee Daily Review 14, August 1909 page 8

**Wright, Coler:** An African-American who was arrested for living off ill-famed women.
"Undesirables Take French Leave" Bisbee Daily Review 25, July 1909 page 7

**Wright, Lorenzo:** Constable in 1911. He arrested a girl dancing nearly nude in the red-light district. With difficulty caused by her lack of clothing and by using backstreets he was able to get her to the justice courts.
"Gave Skirt Dance without the Skirt" Bisbee Daily Review 30, April 1912 page 8

**Womacks, F.J.:** He resided at #33 Brewery Gulch and was hospitalized in 1909 with a scalp injury. Dora Tyson was listed as his friend.

Copper Queen Hospital Patients Register July 18, 1909 Bisbee Mining and Historical Museum, Bisbee

**Woods, J.A.:** Was arrested in near the People's Theater by Officers Wilmoth and Officer Johnson. Woods tried to get away and Wilmoth grabbed Wood's hand that held a .32 caliber pistol. The fight ended when Johnson placed his revolver at Wood's belly.
"Threatens Officers" Bisbee Daily Review 26, May 1906 page 8

**Wortman, William:** He was the husband of Cora Miles and helped her operate her house. Both William and Cora were arrested for defacing an American flag after they attached an ad to the flag. He died in Benson, Arizona of tuberculosis in 1908. William was buried in Evergreen Cemetery at Bisbee.
"Defaced U.S. Flag is Charge" Bisbee Daily Review 19, March 1908 page 5
"Will Wortman Dies" Bisbee Daily Review 21, July 1908 page 7

**Wurst, Adam:** This man was arrested for vagrancy in 1909.
"Raid Nets Nine Undesirable Citizens" Bisbee Daily Review 4, August 1909 page 1

French postcard c- 1910

**Young, Charles B.:** In 1909, Charles an assistant boilermaker was attacked by Gordon Parham and seriously slashed on the neck and face. The incident occurred in an upstairs room at the Little Casino.
<sub>Copper Queen Hospital Patients Register October 13, 1909 Bisbee Mining and Historical Museum, Bisbee.</sub>
"Cutting Affray in Redlight District" <u>Bisbee Daily Review</u> 13, March 1909 page 1
"Young has Good Chance to Recover" <u>Bisbee Daily Review</u> 14, March 1909 page 8

**Young, Oscar:** A 53-year-old cook at a dinner in the red-light district. He died after falling from a porch on his restaurant behind Rose Miller's Place. Oscar was African-American and from Washington D.C.
"Cochise County Coroner's Inquest #9" Arizona State Archives Phoenix

*Zeigler, Charles:* He was known to be a friend of a red-light girl called Maud.
"Zeigler Punched Sax" <u>Bisbee Daily Review</u> 2, August 1903 page 5

French postcard c- 1910

# Appendix

# Timeline

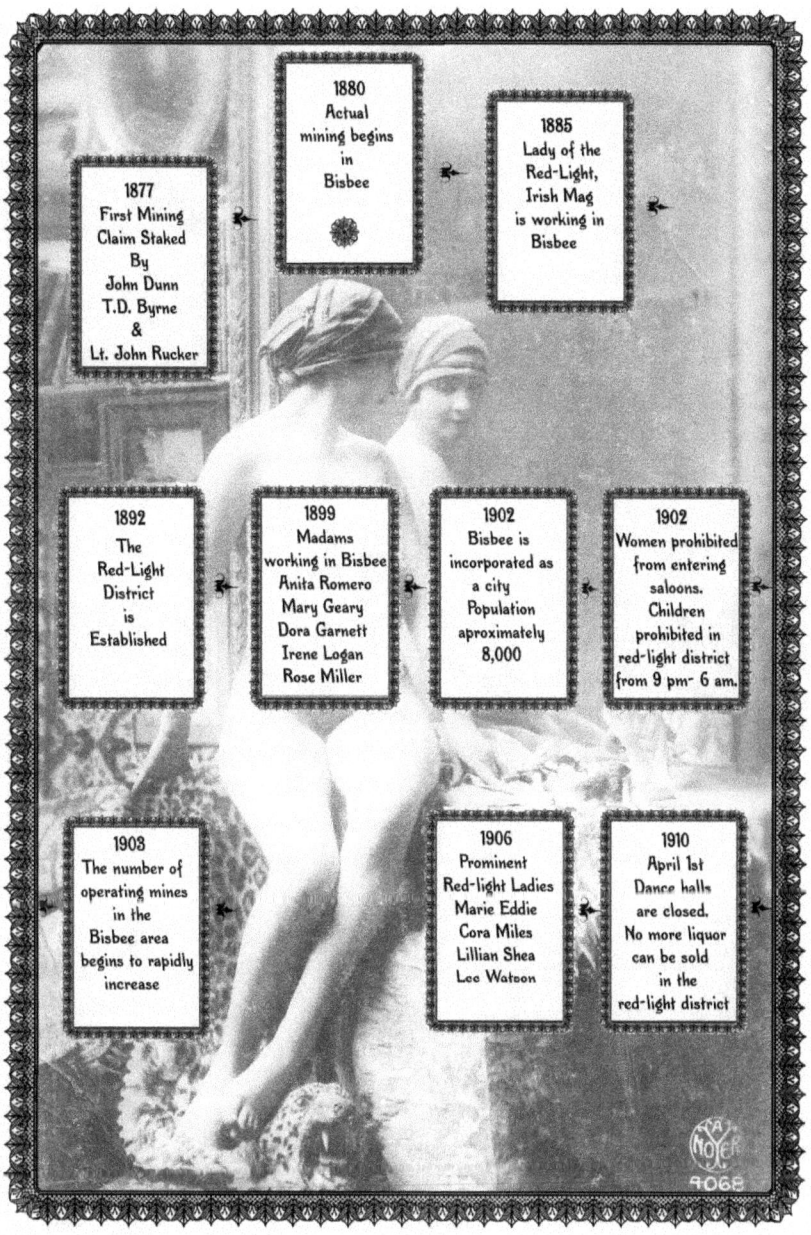

**1877** First Mining Claim Staked By John Dunn T.D. Byrne & Lt. John Rucker

**1880** Actual mining begins in Bisbee

**1885** Lady of the Red-Light, Irish Mag is working in Bisbee

**1892** The Red-Light District is Established

**1899** Madams working in Bisbee Anita Romero Mary Geary Dora Garnett Irene Logan Rose Miller

**1902** Bisbee is incorporated as a city Population aproximately 8,000

**1902** Women prohibited from entering saloons. Children prohibited in red-light district from 9 pm- 6 am.

**1903** The number of operating mines in the Bisbee area begins to rapidly increase

**1906** Prominent Red-light Ladies Marie Eddie Cora Miles Lillian Shea Lee Watson

**1910** April 1st Dance halls are closed. No more liquor can be sold in the red-light district

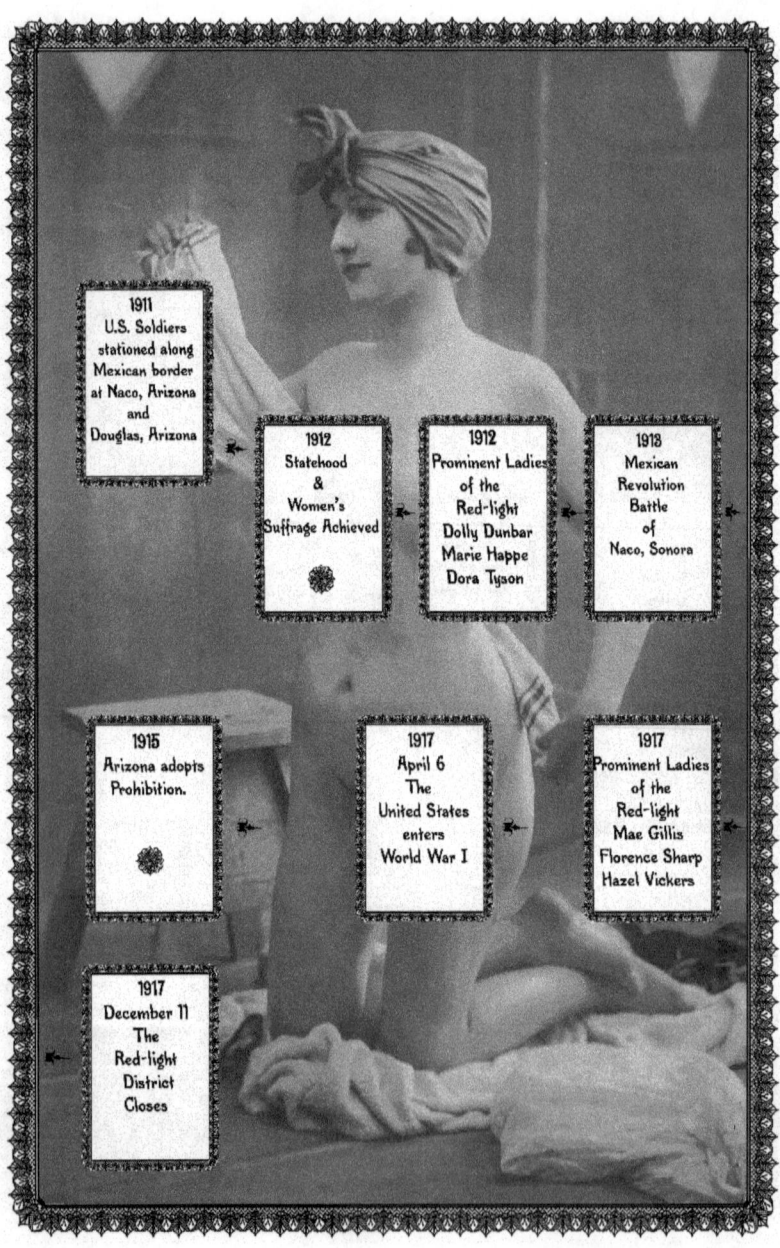

# Euphemisms as applied to Bisbee's red-light district

Many of the primary documents, describe the activities and people of the red-light district with euphanisms or "*A polite way of conveying a disagreeable thing or situation without sounding vulgar*". Only rarely are the women referred to as prostitutes and only in legal documents. This was an attempt at political correctness. Yet, even the girls themselves preferred to call themselves by gentler terms. Below is a quote from the coroner's inquest of Bernard Wilson a soldier killed in the nearby red-light district at Douglas Arizona.

*"Anna Vargas having been called as witness herein, after being duly sworn, testified as follows:-*

*Examination by Mr. Stephenson.*
*Q. State your name?*
*A. Anna Vargas.*
*Q. What is your occupation?*
*A. Well, you know what my occupation is.*
*Q. I know, but that will not do the record any good,. I want it so I can use it if you are not here, the law requires that certains questions be asked and this is one of them?*
*A. Put it down something, domestic"*

# List of Euphemisms

**The Red-light District as a whole**

*Half World*

*Reservation*

*Restricted district*

*Tenderloin*

*The Bad-lands*

*Segregated District*

*Upper Brewery Gulch (not always indicates ill-famed district)*

*Up the Line*

*Darktown (only part of the ill-famed district)*

**As applied to houses of ill-repute**

*Assignation house*

*Bawdy House*

*City Resort*

*Disorderly House (sometimes could refer to a rough saloon)*

*Hog Ranch*

*House of Assignation*

*House of Ill-Fame*

*Resort (sometimes referred to a saloon)*

*House of Ill-Repute*

**As applied to the women**

*Habitués*

*Cyprian*

*Denizens*

*Inmates*

*Apaches*

*Scarlet Lady*

*Soiled Dove*

*Bawdy Lady*

*Ill-Famed Woman*

*Fallen Woman*

*Damsels (applied sarcastically)*

*Woman of the Half World*

*Sporting Woman*

**Terms the ladies applied to themselves**

*Domestic*

*House Keeper*

*Chambermaid*

*Housemaid*

*Milliner*

*Dressmaker*

Dressmaker c-1912

A French postcard illustrated by Xavier Sagar, note he refers to the ill-famed ladies as "*Apaches*" c-1914

Saloon District #1, better known as Main Street c-1902

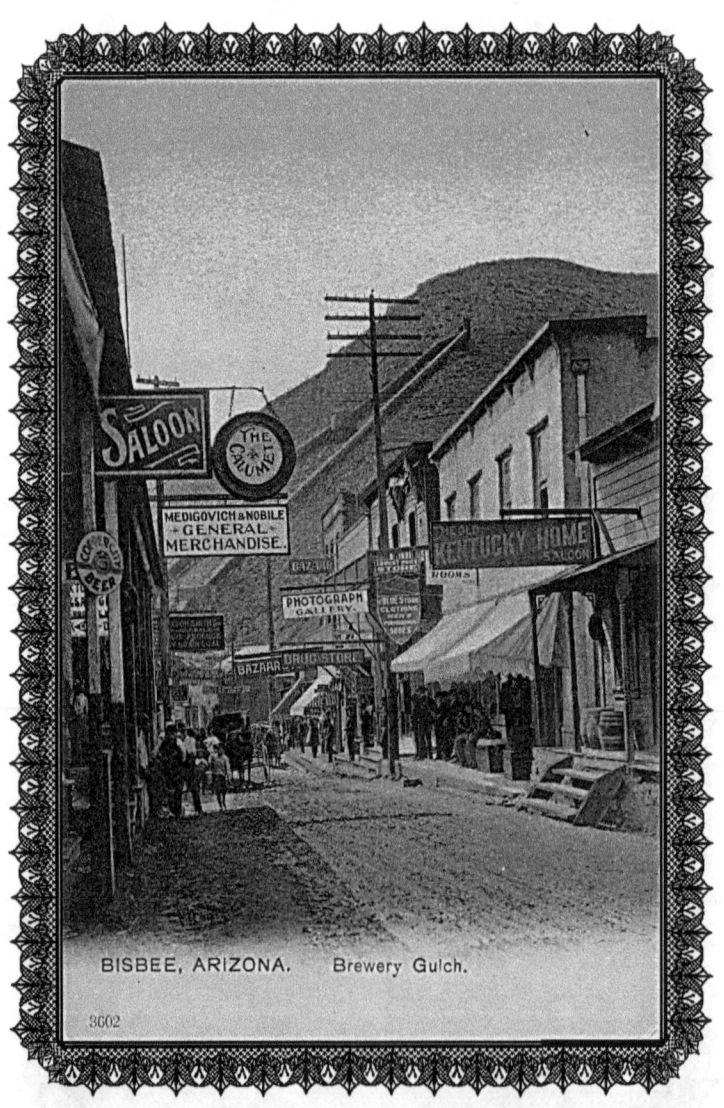

Saloon District #2 or Brewery Gulch, c-1902

Red-light District A view of the southern boundary looking into the district C-1910

The first of three known photographs of the red-light district during the period of legal operation. C-1910 (Bisbee Mining & Historical Museum Collection)

The second known image taken after the 1910 flood (Bisbee Mining & Historical Museum collection)

The third photograph taken shortly before the district closed c-1916 (New Jersey State Archives Collection)

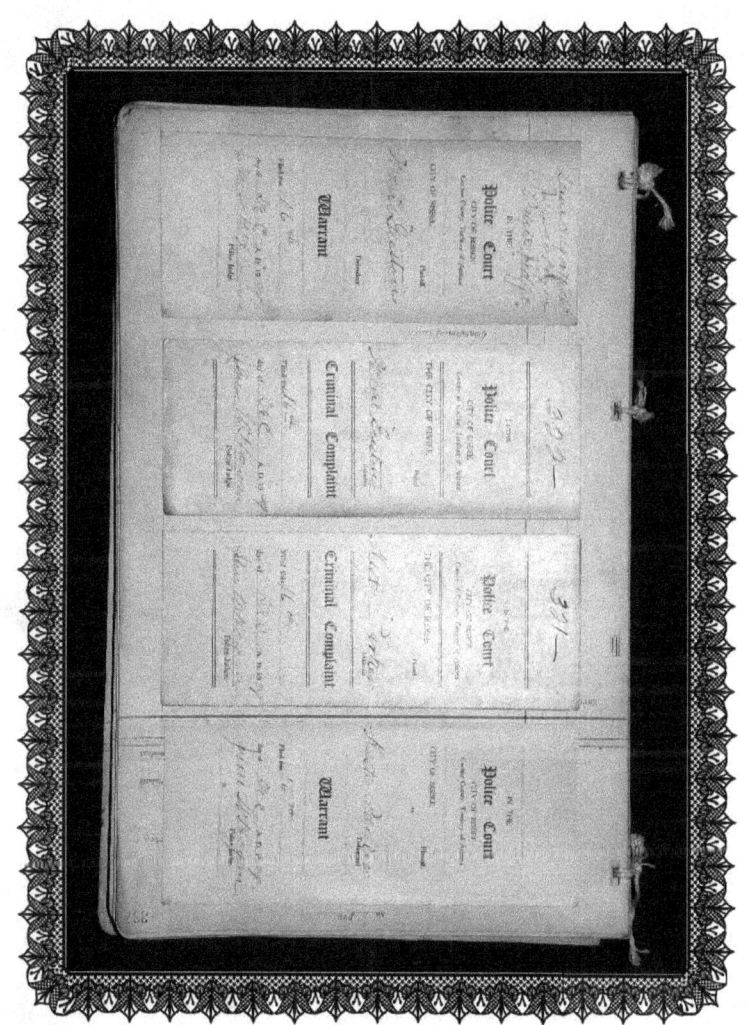

Justice court documents for the fight between Marie Gusten and Hester Parker on December 16, 1909. Note, on the document on the far left it is written " Serve Day or Night"

An interior view of the court documents from the brawl on September 7th 1909

Licenses to dispense medicinal opium & coca leaves for Bisbee dentists.

# Fashions of the Red-light

French postcard of a late Edwardian lady in lingerie. C-1914

# Late Victorian 1880-1899

Irish Mag and a youthful Clara Allen would have been dressed as Victorians.

Late Victorian dresses at this time consisted of an upper section or long-waisted bodice decorated with lace flowing down the front. The sleeves were often puffed at the shoulders and the sleeves were long, snug fitting and ended with delicate lace decoration at the wrists. Delicate collars extended high onto the neck. Skirts were often relatively plain and were tightly fitted at the waist. The bustle that was prominent in earlier Victorian styles had largely ceased to be popular. Although, the photographs disguise the original colors, late Victorian wore bright colors with strong contrasts. Heliotrope (violet shade) and yellow were popular colors.

Late Victorian Hats

With the decline of the bonnet, Late Victorians adopted small hats. These hats were worn high on the head and generally straight. They were lavishly decorated and sometimes included feathered wings small birds and even beetles.

Late Victorian Hairstyle

The long hair was often the pride of a Victorian woman. It was carefully fashioned into bun with lavish curls exposed on the forehead. Sometimes the hair would be allowed to flow down the back or onto a shoulder.

# Early Edwardian Style

This is the fashion style of madams, like, Anita Romero, Dora Garnett, Mary Geary and Rose Miller.

The stiffness of the Victorian gave way to the graceful figure of the Edwardian. The use of a long straight fronted corset gave the ladies an "S" curve. Emphasizing the bosom and the posterior. Muslin, Chiffon and gauze were common materials to form outfits. The colors were pale with intense embroidery. Collars were still extended high up the neck.

Early Edwardian Hats

The tiny hats were soon replaced by massive hat wear that was lavishly decorated, often with ostrich feathers, flowers and even birds. Long ornate hat pins secured the hats to the lady's hair

Early Edwardian Hair Style

Hair was waved in the front and elevated by a rat made of hair lost during brushing. Extra hair pieces were often added to complete a pompadour.

# Late Edwardian Style

The last of Bisbee's red-light girls, like Irene Brown, May Gillis and Florence Sharp would have dressed themselves in such fashion.

    The dresses flowed around the natural form of the woman creating a vertical slender look in contrast to the forced "S" curve of the Early Edwardians. The dresses had a light, airy, delicate appearance. Collars became lower exposing the neckline.

As the Edwardian period approached an end, hats were still large, but the decoration was simplified. The coming streamlined features of the following Art Deco are becoming evident. Hat pins were still popular, but would fade out of fashion with the introduction of smaller hats.

The long hair prized by the Victorians and Early Edwardians began to fall to scissors. In anticipation of the oncoming Art Deco, bobs became fashionable with younger women. Waved with early versions of the curling iron, these hairdos were often accented with hairbands of luxurious fabrics decorated with detailed stitching and beading.

An Xavier Sagar postcard mailed in 1913 comparing the different styles between the 1880's and the 1910's

**Copper Queen Store women's clothing cost for 1899**

Skirts $1.25- $2.75

Store Women's shoes $1.00- $2.00

Shirt waists $.50- $1.25

Jackets $7.00- $17.50

Capes $7.50- $13.50

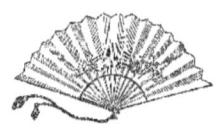
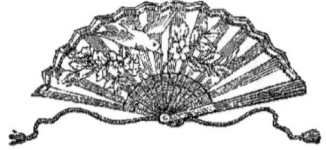

**Copper Queen Store women's clothing cost for 1904**

Shirt waists $ .95- $ 4.75

Underskirts $.95- $2.95

Wash skirts $1.00- $3.75

Hats $3.50- $25.00

Hosiery $.35-$3.00

Shoes $.80-$2.25

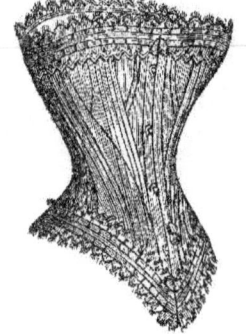

## Copper Queen Store women's clothing cost for 1907

Coats $7.50- $65.00

Hats $2.50- $10.00 on sale

Furs Mink, Blue Lynx, Squirrel, Fox $ 5.25- $25.00

Suits, $20.00- $22.50

Under wear, $ .60- $.95

Coats from $5.00- $43.50

Sweaters $1.25- $3.00

Skirts $4.00- $12.00

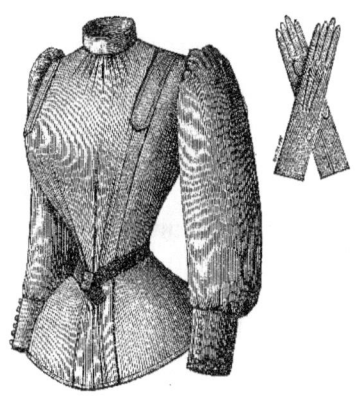

## Copper Queen Store women's clothing cost for 1909

Skirts from $4.50- $15.00

Hats from $3.35-$20.00

Petticoat $4.50-$18.75

Suits $12.00- $30.00

**Phelps Dodge Mercantile**

**(Copper Queen Store) women's clothing cost for 1912**

Tailored suits $13.00-$20.25

Wool dresses $3.50-$22.25

Winter coats $10.75-$22.50

Silk dresses $5.50-$22.25

Evening gowns $15.00-$27.50

**Phelps Dodge Mercantile**

**(Copper Queen Store) women's clothing cost for 1916**

Suits $7.50- $32.50

Street dresses $7.95 - $45.00

Evening gowns $9.38-$67.50

Winter coats $5.22-$48.75

Hats $3.95 & $6.95

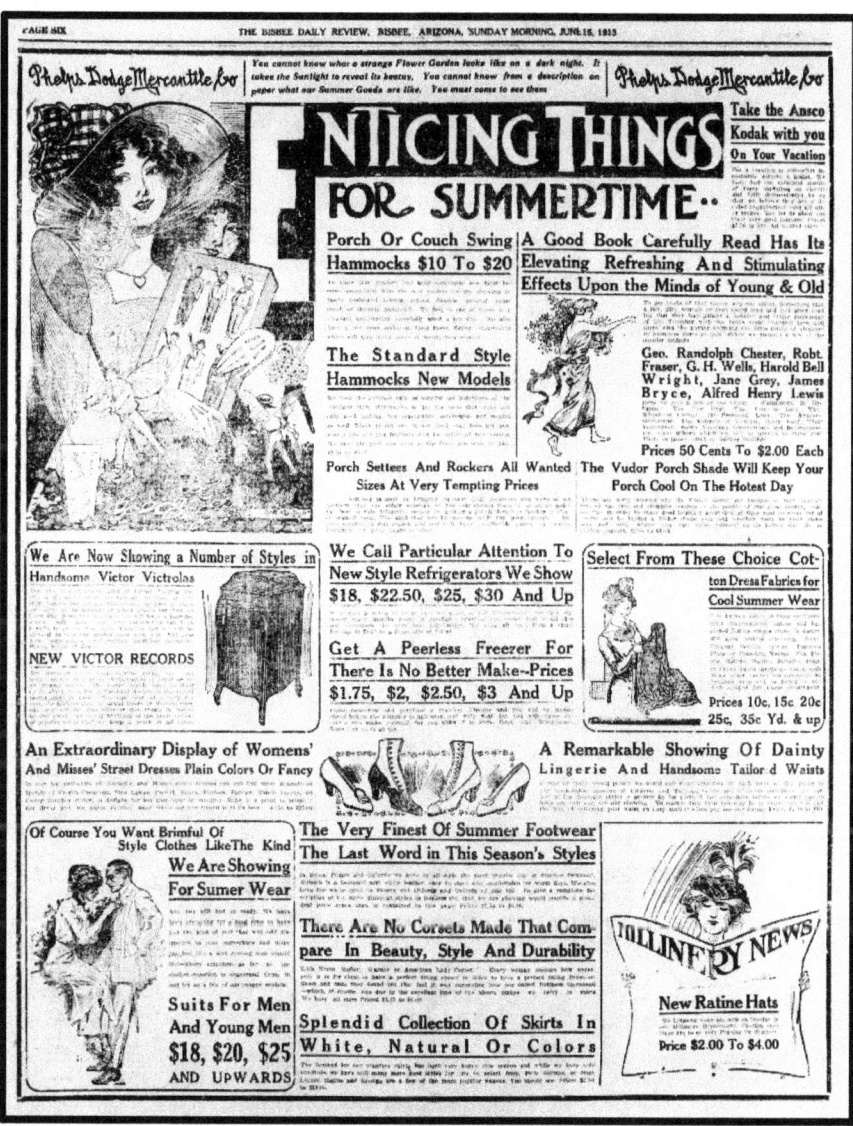

Newspaper ad for the Phelps Dodge Mercantile in Bisbee.

Main Street Bisbee C-1885. This is how Bisbee appeared when Irish Mag was a member of the community. (Courtesy Bisbee Mining & Historical Museum)

Main Street, around 1895. This was the Bisbee of Anita Romero, Irene Logan, Dora Garnett and Mary Geary

Main Street, c-1905, Cora Miles and the Shea's were operating houses at this time.

Main Street, c-1910 Dolly Dunbar, May Gillis, Marie Happe and Dora Tyson were prominent members of the red-light district in this period.

Main Street, c-1917, the last of the madams of the legal period such as Mae Scott and Florence Sharp are operating houses

# Coroners' Inquest for Ethel Paterson October 16, 1911

French postcard c-1908

IN THE CORONER'S OFFICE OF PRECINCT NUMBER TWO,
IN AND FOR THE COUNTY OF COCHISE, TERRITORY OF ARIZONA.
BEFORE M. C. HIGH, CORONER EX-OFFICIO.

IN THE MATTER OF THE INQUISITION :
UPON THE BODY OF -
    Ethel Paterson,     : Witnesses examined:
           Deceased.

870

DR. N. C. BLEDSOE, BEING CALLED AS A WITNESS HEREIN, HAVING BEEN FIRST DULY SWORN ACCORDING TO LAW, WAS EXAMINED AND TESTIFIED AS FOLLOWS:

Q What is your name and occupation?
A N. C. Bledsoe; physician and surgeon.
Q In her life time, did you know this person upon whom we are holding this inquisition?
A I did not.
Q Were you called upon to make an examination of the body?
A I was.
Q Will you state to the Jury what you discovered by your examination and the cause of her death as nearly as you could determine it?
A I found the body in the O. K. Undertaking Parlors and upon an examination of the body, I found that there had been a slight bruise to the left side of the face and a little ecchymosis, or "black eye", behind the left eye. Upon the lips and tongue, there were decided evidences of some escharotic poison -- I mean one that burns -- and from the character of it, and by opening the abdomen, I found the stomach to be full of a fluid which had distinctly the smell of carbolic acid and the stomach lining was also very much inflamed from the escharotic poison and I take it

216

that her death was due to poisoning by carbolic acid.

-- (Witness excused.) --

---

MAUD HUNT, BEING CALLED AS A WITNESS HEREIN, HAVING BEEN FIRST DULY SWORN ACCORDING TO LAW, WAS EXAMINED AND TESTIFIED AS FOLLOWS:

Q   What is your name?
A   Maud Hunt.
Q   Where do you reside?
A   At Marie Happy's, No. 9 Brewery Gulch.
Q   In Bisbee?
A   Yes sir.
Q   In her life time did you know this Ethel Paterson, upon whom we are holding this inquisition?
A   I did.
Q   How long have you known her?
A   I have known her for about a month.
Q   Were you living in the same house with her?
A   Yes sir.
Q   Did you see her yesterday?
A   Yes sir.
Q   Were you at the house when her death occurred?
A   I was in my room.
Q   Had you seen her during the day?
A   She was in my room about half an hour yesterday evening.
Q   At what time was that?
A   About four o'clock.
Q   Where had she been in the afternoon?
A   She had been in her room all afternoon until about 4:30 or 5:00 when she took and buggy and went somewhere.
Q   Who was with her in the buggy?

A     I don't know; I didn't see her when she left.

Q     Did you see her after she came back in the buggy?

A     No sir.

Q     What conversation, if any, did you hold with her?

A     Nothing. I had been for a walk and she came in and asked me where I went and things like that and walked on out.

Q     Did she seem to be disheartened?

A     She seemed like she was kind of blue.

Q     Were you intimately acquainted with her?

A     I have lived right there with her for the last month -- since I have been in Bisbee.

Q     You didn't see her after she came back with the buggy?

A     No sir.

Q     Were you in her room after it happened?

A     As soon as we heard her throw the bottle out in the hall, we all rushed in there about the same time.

Q     You went in there after you heard the bottle?

A     Yes sir.

Q     In what condition was she then?

A     She was kind of having a spasm or something like that.

Q     Did she say anything?

A     No sir, she didn't say anything.

Q     What did you do after you got into her room?

A     She fell off the bed and me and two other girls put her back on the bed and she just laid there and didn't make another move.

Q     Did you get a doctor?

A     One of the girls run after a doctor and someone ran up to #33 after some alcohol. Then we began to pour milk down until the doctor came.

Q     She never said a word?

A     No sir.

Q     Do you know of any message that she left behind?

A   She left a little note, but we couldn't make it out; it was all torn up.

Q   Is this the note? (Two pieces of white paper exhibited written in pencil).

A   Yes sir.

Q   Where was this note when you first saw it?

A   Marie had it. Somebody had already given it to her then.

Q   Is this the bottle that you saw up there? (A small two ounce bottle exhibited).

A   Yes sir, or one like it.

Q   Where was that bottle when you got into the room?

A   She had thrown it out into the hall.

Q   Did she have the door open?

A   Yes sir.

Q   Had you seen that bottle before?

A   No sir.

Q   Did you never see any carbolic acid in the room before?

A   She never did have it around before.

Q   Did she ever make any threats about taking her life?

A   She never did around me.

Q   She seemed to be pleasant always?

A   Always -- all the time.

-- (Witness excused.) --

------------------o------------------

MARIE HAPPY, BEING CALLED AS A WITNESS HEREIN, HAVING BEEN FIRST DULY SWORN ACCORDING TO LAW, WAS EXAMINED AND TESTIFIED AS FOLLOWS:

Q   What is your name?

A   Marie Happy.

Q   Where do you reside?

A   At No. 9, Brewery Gulch, in Bisbee.

Q   In her life time did you know this Ethel Paterson, upon whom we are holding this inquisition?

A   I have known her for about a year.

-- 4 --

Q   Was she residing in your house?
A   Yes sir.
Q   Had she been living there for a year?
A   She came out here about a year ago next month and she stayed for a few months and went back to Texas, and then she came back about July and has been with me ever since.
Q   Were you very intimate friends?
A   She was my best friend.
Q   What is her full name?
A   Ethel Paterson is all I know.
Q   About how old was she?
A   About twenty years old.
Q   Where was she born, if you know?
A   She was born in Austin, Texas.
Q   Do you know if her parents are living?
A   Her father is and she has a stepmother.
Q   Her mother is not living?
A   No, her mother is dead.
Q   Do you know her father's name?
A   Joe R. Clough.
Q   Was she a married woman?
A   Yes; she has a child four years old.
Q   Is her husband living?
A   They are separated, but I don't know whether divorced or not.
Q   Did you see her yesterday afternoon?
A   I was sick in bed all day yesterday and I'll tell you what I know about it. She had all-night company Saturday night and went to bed -- a Slavonian stayed all night. She came down in the evening and turned her money in and went upstairs and later one of her friends came and asked for her. In the morning I went up to call her and the fellow that was in the

-- 5 --

room told me to come in. I went into the room and
I didn't see Ethel and he was alone; so I asked him
where Ethel was. He says: "Ethel is gone." I says:
"Where has she gone?" He says: "I don't know."
She had been in the habit of going to a certain place
where I have begged and begged her not to go and I
talked to her Saturday about not going there. Where
she went I don't know, but in my own mind I'm pretty
well satisfied. I was sick in bed all day yesterday and at dinner time, five o'clock, I went up to
her room to get her to come down and eat something.
One of the girls said she had not been in her room.
I don't know what time she came home. When I went
up to her room -- I could always do anything with her
that I wanted to if she had been drinking but she had
not been drinking then --, I asked her if she would
not come down and have some dinner, but she said no.
We had a good chicken dinner, things that she liked,
but she would not come down. I asked her if I could
bring her dinner up to her -- she's always stubborn
that way, -- but no. So I left her alone and after
dinner I went back to bed and then I went to sleep.
Mabel, one of the girls there, woke me saying that
Ethel had taken carbolic acid, so I got up. Before
I went to her room, I telephoned for Dr. Miner; then
I 'phoned the Chief of Police, and when I went into
the room, she was dying. She said: "Don't do anything for me; I'm dying and I want to die." That's
all she said. About ten days ago, she asked me what
I'd do if a girl should die in my house. I told her
I would do the best I could for her. "Well", she
says, "we all have to die and if it wasn't for my
baby, I would have been dead long ago." Last

-- 6 --

Monday she asked me -- she didn't have any money --
if I wouldn't give her some money to buy her baby
some clothes with. So we went to The Fair and
bought several little things and I paid for them,
and on Tuesday we sent the express package away to
the baby (four years old) for his birthday present.
She didn't have any money, so I put a little money
in the pockets for her. She wrote a little note
and sent it to her step-mother and asked her to give
it to him. Yesterday when the girls called me, she
told me that she wanted to die -- not to do anything
for her; but we did everything that we could but
could not save her.

Q Did you at any time think that she was under the influence of a drug?

A I forgot to tell you that she came into my room yesterday and asked Mr. Happy for $2.00. Happy started to give it to her, when she asked: "What's a buggy on Sunday -- $1.50, isn't it?" "$2.50, I think," he said, "maybe $3.00." So he gave her $3.00. Then after dinner I went to sleep and didn't know anything about it until the girls came and called me, saying that she was dying.

Q Do you know who she was out with in the buggy?

A She went alone the girls said that saw her leave the house. Mabel was on the porch. She went alone and came back alone. I think she took the buggy and went and bought the bottle of stuff.

Q Do you know how long she was gone?

A I was asleep when she came back. I expect Mabel would know if anybody would.

Q Is that all that you know in regard to it?

A Yes sir.

Q Is that the note she wrote? (same pieces of paper as formerly exhibited.)

A    That's the note. I don't know where I got it. I don't know whether I picked it up or whether it was handed to me. One is always kind of excited, you know, but when I got it, it was all crumpled up and torn.

Q    What does that note say?

A    As I read it: "Dear Marie: Please don't send my body home. ********* ---- he will bury me." -- We compared it last night, the Chief and I. Some of it is gone.

Q    Evidently the name of someone is torn out?

A    Yes. One of the girls says that she wrote it earlier in the evening and then tore it up.

Q    And you don't know whether you picked it up or whether it was handed to you?

A    No, I don't know how I got it. -- because I was crazy.

Q    Is that the bottle that was found? (same bottle exhibited)

A    Yes sir.

Q    Where was it found?

A    When I first saw it, somebody had picked it up from the floor in the hall.

Q    Did she scream after she had taken the poison?

A    No.

Q    And all she said is what you have stated?

A    Yes. Her throat was all swollen then. She said: "Don't do anything for me, Marie, for I want to die."

-- (Witness excused.) --

----------------------O------------------

Dr. L. L. MINER, BEING CALLED AS A WITNESS HEREIN, HAVING BEEN FIRST DULY SWORN ACCORDING TO LAW, WAS EXAMINED AND TESTIFIED AS FOLLOWS:

Q    What is your name and occupation?

A    L. L. Miner; physician.

Q    In her life time, did you know this Ethel Paterson, upon whom we are holding this inquisition?

A    I saw her a few days before her death.

Q    Were you called upon to administer to her at any time?

A    I was, last night.

Q    Just tell the Jury everything that you know in regard to it?

A    Somewhere close to seven o'clock last night, I got a telephone call stating that a girl at No. 9 had taken carbolic acid and asking me to come up and take care of her. When I got there, it was apparent that she was not going to live very long. Every attempt was made to get rid of the carbolic acid, but it was impossible. She lived, I should say, probably about thirty minutes, and then died.

Q    Did she speak?

A    No, she was unconscious when I got there.

Q    Did you see this bottle, doctor? (bottle exhibited).

A    I presume that is the same bottle.

Q    What size is this bottle?

A    It is a two ounce bottle.

-- (Witness excused.) --

OSCAR DOYLE, BEING CALLED AS A WITNESS HEREIN, HAVING BEEN FIRST DULY SWORN ACCORDING TO LAW, WAS EXAMINED AND TESTIFIED AS FOLLOWS:

Q    What is your name and occupation?

A    Oscar Doyle; druggist.

Q    In her life time, did you know this Ethel Paterson upon whom we are holding this inquisition?

A    No, I did not know her.

Q    Have you ever seen her that you know of?

A    No, not that I know of.

Q    Has anyone that you know of bought any carbolic acid in your place of business?

A   I'll just tell you in a few words. Yesterday afternoon
    -- just what time I don't know, but it was between
    half past five and half past six -- a buggy drove up
    in front of the Drug Store at Lowell; it didn't
    drive quite up in front of the store. Mrs. John
    was in the store at the time. Just as I got to the
    door, a lady jumped out of the buggy and was coming in.
    When she came into the door, I said "Good evening" and
    she said "Good evening", and she says: "I would like
    to purchase a bar of carbolic soap." I tried to find
    it for her, but I could not, so I told her: "I'm
    very sorry, lady, but I can't find any carbolic soap."
    She says: "Well, just give me two bits worth of
    carbolic acid; that will do." She was very uncon-
    cerned about it and said it in a businesslike way,
    so that one would never dream of anything out of the
    way. She was looking around the store while I put
    the medicine up (carbolic acid) and when I came around
    and handed it to her, I said: "Now, lady, you want
    to be very, very careful; this is full strength and
    a very powerful drug." "Yes", she said, "I will."
    I asked her if there was anything else she wanted.
    "No, thank you", she said and I said "Good evening"
    and she went out. I wouldn't know the lady.

Q   Was she tall?

A   Probably a little taller than I am. I didn't pay much
    attention to her; so many people come into the
    store. -- That's all that I know about it, Judge.

Q   Was she alone in the buggy?

A   I don't think she was. I think there was a gentleman in
    the buggy with her. I didn't pay very close atten-
    tion to it, but I think there was someone in the

buggy with her. There was nothing in the appearance of the woman that would indicate suspicion in any way, shape, or form. She asked for it in a businesslike way.

-- (Witness excused.) --

C. F. HAPPY, BEING CALLED AS A WITNESS HEREIN, HAVING BEEN FIRST DULY SWORN ACCORDING TO LAW, WAS EXAMINED AND TESTIFIED AS FOLLOWS:

Q What is your name?
A C. F. Happy.
Q Where do you reside?
A In No. 9, Brewery Gulch.
Q In her lifetime, did you know this Ethel Paterson, upon whom we are now holding this inquisition?
A Yes, I have known her for about a year, I guess.
Q Was she stopping at the same house where you are?
A Yes sir.
Q Did you see her yesterday?
A Yes sir, right after breakfast, about one o'clock; she came from across the street. Later in the afternoon she came to me and asked me for $2.00. She says: "What does a buggy cost on Sunday? $1.50 isn't it?" "No", I says, "I think it is $2.50." "Well", she says, "then you better give me $3.00." So I gave her $3.00 and she turned around and walked out.
Q When did you see her next?
A One of the girls hollered down to Mabel and said: "For God's sake get a doctor; Ethel has taken poison." We didn't have any alcohol in the house, so I sent one of the girls to #33 after some. We gave her

-- 11 --

some of that and by that time someone else came.

  Then the doctor came, but I didn't stay around much.

Q  Did you think that she was under the influence of opiates or anything of that kind at any time?

A  She was unconscious when I saw her.

Q  You don't know who was out in the buggy with her?

A  I didn't see her leave or come back.

Q  Do you know who picked up that note?

A  Mr. Watkins showed it to me. We compared the paper with the length in her writing pad. Some seemed to be torn off -- about half an inch or three-quarters. That was the first I saw of it.

-- (Witness excused.) --

---------------------0-------------------

MABEL CARRINGTON, BEING CALLED AS A WITNESS HEREIN, HAVING BEEN FIRST DULY SWORN ACCORDING TO LAW, WAS EXAMINED AND TESTIFIED AS FOLLOWS:

Q  What is your name?

A  Mabel Carrington.

Q  Where do you reside?

A  No. 9, Brewery Gulch, Bisbee.

Q  In her life time, did you know this Ethel Paterson?

A  Yes sir.

Q  How long have you known her?

A  For about six weeks.

Q  Was she stopping in the same house that you are?

A  Yes sir.

Q  Did you see her yesterday afternoon?

A  Yes sir.

Q  What condition did she seem to be in yesterday afternoon? Did she seem to be under the influence of drugs?

A  I don't know, but she talked kind of funny. I asked her to go horseback riding with me, but she said she was going somewhere else by herself. While she

- 12 -

        stayed on the front steps waiting for the buggy, she said that she was going to kill herself.

Q   She told you she would kill herself?

A   Yes sir.

Q   About what time was that?

A   It must have been about six o'clock. I went upstairs just as the buggy came. I don't know whether she was alone or not, but I think a helper at the stable drove her down. She was not gone but ten or fifteen minutes.

Q   What else did she say?

A   Nothing else. I didn't think she meant what she said. Girls lots of times say what they don't mean. I never thought she meant it; I thought she was just joshing.

Q   That was before the buggy came?

A   Yes, she had her wraps on, waiting for the buggy.

Q   Do you know where she had been during the afternoon?

A   No, I don't; I saw her coming out of her room.

Q   Had she made such threats before?

A   I never heard them before.

Q   Who was in the room first after she took the poison?

A   I couldn't say. When I heard her throw the bottle -- as soon as I heard it hit the hall -- I ran to the room and saw the bottle in the hall and I hollered to the girls to get a doctor and that Ethel had taken carbolic acid. When I got into the room, I says: "Ethel, what have you taken?" and she says: "I've taken carbolic acid because I want to die."

Q   Did she seem to be in pain?

A   She had convulsions and fell off the bed. We put her back on the bed and she never made another move.

Q   Did she seem to have any trouble or worry on her mind?

A   I have been out several times with her, but she never

mentioned anything to me.

-- (Witness excused.) --

---o---

VERN LA MORE, BEING CALLED AS A WITNESS HEREIN, HAVING BEEN FIRST DULY SWORN ACCORDING TO LAW, WAS EXAMINED AND TESTIFIED AS FOLLOWS:

Q   What is your name?
A   Vern La More.
Q   In her life time, did you know this Ethel Paterson?
A   Yes sir.
Q   Did you see her yesterday?
A   Yes sir.
Q   Where did you see her?
A   At No. 9, Brewery Gulch.
Q   Were you there at the time she took the poison?
A   I was on the steps when she took it.
Q   Did you see her during the afternoon?
A   Yes sir.
Q   Where did you see her?
A   At No. 9, Brewery Gulch.
Q   Did you have any conversation with her during the afternoon?
A   None to speak of, no sir.
Q   Did she seem to have worry on her mind?
A   When I saw her yesterday afternoon, she was in the Canadian Club. She sent for me to come over there. I went over. She was lying down with her eyes sticking out of her head and she didn't seem to have any life about her. When we started away from there, she seemed to be fainting, so I picked her up and carried her over to No. 9. She seemed awfully funny. I talked to her quite a little while up in her room. She told me she had been using "coke",

-- 14 --

and I told her I didn't think it was right. But she
said she didn't care. Then I went down town and
came back and I saw her coming up in the buggy.
Later we heard the girls holler and we ran up there
and found she had taken carbolic acid.

Q Who was with her in the buggy, do you know?
A I noticed a man in white shirt. They had a Palace horse, and I think, the man was a helper over there.
Q Have you seen this note before?
A I never looked at it personally, but I have seen it.
Q You don't know where the note was found?
A No sir.

-- (Witness excused.) --

IN THE CORONER'S OFFICE OF NUMBER _Two_ PRECINCT,
Cochise County, Arizona Territory.

----oOo----

In the Matter of the Inquisition
Upon the Body of
_Ethel Paterson_
Deceased.

CORONER'S CERTIFICATE.

I, _M. C. Heigh_, Coroner Ex-Officio of Number _Two_ Precint, County of Cochise, Territory of Arizona, do hereby certify that I held an Inquisition upon the body of _Ethel Paterson_, a native of _Texas_, aged about _20_ years, at _Bisbee_, Arizona, on the _16th_ day of _Oct_, A. D. 19_11_.

VERDICT OF THE CORONER'S JURY:

_Carbolic Acid poison -- Taken with Suicidal intent._

And I further certify that I ordered the remains removed to _O. K. Undertaking Parlors_

Given under my hand at _Bisbee_, Arizona, this _16th_ day of _Oct_, A.D._1911_

_M. C. Heigh_
Coroner Ex-Officio.

## Ill-famed ladies from around Cochise County and bordering Mexican communities

### Red-light ladies working at Agua Prieta, Sonora, Mexico

Arreola, Concepcion, 1909

Arreola, Maria, 1909

Cardenas, Rosa, 1909

Lopez, Pilar, 1909

Marquez, Elena, 1909

Moreno, Maria, 1909

Mungaray, Josefa, 1909

Rothenhauser, Teresa, 1909

### Red-light ladies working at Cananea, Sonora, Mexico. This mining community had strong ties to Bisbee. Many families had relatives in both cities. Travel between the cities was common.

Afielda, Lucy, 1909

Aguirre, Ines, 1909

Aguayo, Concepcion, 1909

Allen, Minnie, 1909

Aoki, Maria, 1909

Akoi, Rina, 1909

Arvizu, Ana, 1909

Avendano, Maria R., 1909

Backer, Stella, 1909

Boites, Petra, 1909
Bojorquez, Teresa, 1909
Brun, Dot, 1909
Day, Cora, 1909
Ellsworth, Claire, 1909
Escobosa, Soledad, 1909
Espinosa, Manuela, 1909
Felix, Isabel, 1909
Flores, Ramona, 1909
Franco, Maria, 1909
Galindo, Concepcion, 1909
Galindo, Maria, 1909
Garcia, Ana, 1909
Garcia, Laura, 1909
Garcia, Luisa, 1909
Gastelum, Guadalupe, 1909
Gerol, May, 1909
Gomez Celise, 1909
Gomez, Mariana, 1909
Gonzales, Emilia, 1909
Gray, Josie, 1909
Guevara, Francisca, 1909
Gutierrez, Rosa, 1909
Hale, Lulli, 1909
Harvey, Hazel, 1909
Hazmoto, Yelow, 1909
Hernandez Genoveva, 1909

Camacho, Refugia, 1909
Camou, Dol, 1909

Hopbrod, Monie Z., 1909
Jaime, Jacinta, 1909
Jana, Yse, 1909
Jimenez Aurelia, 1909
Jones, Lilliam, 1909
Jones, Topay, 1909
Jordan, Louise, 1909
Kato, Mary, 1909
Ki, Ku, 1909
Ki, Toma, 1909
Ku, Fie, 1909
Ledesma, Braulia, 1909
Legrande, Angela, 1909
Leon, Carmen, 1909
Lora, Ignacia, 1909
Lopez, Pilar, 1909
Lyions, Bassy, 1909
Machi, Inoyi, 1909
Manuel, Pearl, 1909
Mata, Isabel, 1909
Maturin, Maria, 1909
McCaslin, Clarice, 1909
Moore, Rooth L., 1909
Morgan, Tessae, 1909

Natzi, Jo Ku, 1909

Natzu, Yaku, 1909

Navarro, Loreto, 1909

Oseguera, Isaura, 1909

Osio, Rosario, 1909

Palmbe, Minophe, 1909

Parker, Gertrudis, 1909

Pierce, Lilliam, 1909

Portillo, Jesus, 1909

Preciado, Margarita, 1909

Puga, Ramona, 1909

Pybrun, May, 1909

Ramirez, Ines, 1909

Reyes, Concepcion, 1909

Reyes Trinidad, 1909

Rico, Refugia, 1909

Rios, Concepcion, 1909

Rodriguez, Felicitas, 1909

Romero, Maria, 1909

Ramos, Teresa, 1909

Ruiz, Virginia, 1909

Saba, Akey, 1909

Salazar, Valerina, 1909

Sanchez, Eufemia, 1909

**Red-light ladies working at Courtland, Arizona**

Mrs. Frank Auger, 1909

Sandoval, Rosa, 1909

Santa Cruz, Rosaria, 1909

Smith, Maxime, 1909

Speart, Lena, 1909

Stewart, Nethie, 1909

Spires, Lilliam, 1909

Tamayo Guadalupe, 1909

Temple, Eva, 1909

Toku, O., 1909

Toma, Ki, 1909

Torres, Cayetana, 1909

Torres, Dolores, 1909

Torress Rafaela, 1909

Valencia, Petra, 1909

Valenzuela, Carmen, 1909

Vasquez, Jesus, 1909

Villarino, Luisa, 1909

Villasenor, Cesarea, 1909

Villasenor, Rosario, 1909

Williams, Fay, 1909

Williams, May, 1909

Yanez, Mercedes, 1909

Ybarra, Catalina, 1909

**Red-light ladies working at Douglas, Arizona**

"Beatrice", 1903

*Pearl Phillips, 1903*

*Irene Nevins, 1903*

*"Dot" Sparks, 1906*

*Hamilton, Ollie, 1908*

*Davis, Ruby, 1909 (later moved to Bisbee)*

*Little, Dot, 1909*

*McKay, Maria, 1909*

*Woods, Nellie, 1909*

*Smith, Belle, 1910*

*Wilson, Ada, 1905*

*Livingston, Jennie, 1905*

*Hamilton, Ollie, 1905*

*Gray, May, 1905*

*Newray, Nellie, 1905*

*Short, Maude, 1905*

*Bennetze, Elsie, 1905*

*Thompson, Georgie, 1905*

*Wright, Clara, 1905*

*Wright, Minnie, 1905*

*Miss Jacqueline, 1905*

*Eikler, Pearl, 1907*

*Miss Joaquina Aguila, 1905*

*O'Rea, Rowena, 1905*

*Clark, Claudia, 1909*

*Smith, Belle, 1909*

*Bergess, Fannie, 1909*

*Hughes, Stella, 1905*

*Vance, Irene, 1905*

*Wellington, Willie, 1905*

*Robinson, Lida, 1905*

*Lesper, Jessie, 1905*

*Smith, Daisy, 1905*

*Anderson, Pear, l1905*

*Santacruz, Maria, 1905*

*Gray, Josie, 1905*

*Hamlin, Mabel, 1905*

*Shepard, Minni, 1905*

*Jackson, Mary, 1905*

*Knave, Eva, 1905*

*Horton, Ella, 1905*

*Silues, Ray, 1905*

*Morphine Lill, 1908*

*Earl, Ruby, 1911*

*Wellington, Rose, 1905*

*Ward, F.C. Mrs., 1905*

*Hughes, Stella, 1907*

*Ikner, Pearl, 1907 (from Bisbee)*

*Morey, Emma, 1907*

*Hill, Eva, 1916*

*Hill June, 1916*

*Smith, Alma, 1916*

*Vargas, Anna, 1916*

*Willis, Iva, 1916*

*Martin, Lela, 1916*

*"Pauline", 1909*

*Knight, Clara, 1909*

*Lee, Tessie, 1913*

**Red-light ladies working at Naco, Sonora Mexico in 1907-1909**

*Almada, Jesus*

*Anguiano, Jesus*

*Lopez Natividad*

*Martinez, Carmen*

*Martinez, Maria*

*Ramo, Sofia*

*Ruiz, Maria*

*Valdez, Jesus*

**Red-light ladies working at Tombstone, Arizona**

*Elder, Kate, 1882*

*Mortimer, Emma, 1885*

*Racanzone, Lena, 1909 (Madam of Union Saloon)*

*Mayfield, Mildred, 1907*

An ill-famed lady on 6th St. in Douglas, Arizona

# Ill-famed Hobo of Wilcox

This story was found among the belongings of Watoga Bouidnot of Wilcox, Arizona. after she committed suicide by strychnine poisoning in the red-light district at Globe, Arizona. The tale describes the travels of two red-light girls one Irish and the other of Mexican descent. Watoga was the pretty little Mexican girl. Wilcox is a small town located in Northeastern Cochise County.

June 1910

*"We left Waco, Tex, March 28$^{th}$ on the blind of a baggage car, at 12:50 on the Katy Flier. The porter made us get off at Temple, Tex. But we got on again and stayed until San Antonio at 7:33 am. It was raining and no one in the yards seen us get off. We stayed in San Antonio until the 22$^{nd}$ of April and caught a freight out of there-the Sunset- at the stockyards. There was no place we could ride but a refrigerator car. It was very warm and we had no water with us. There was no one seen us get on as it was 7:40 at night and very dark. We stayed in the car until we arrived at Del Rio, Where we had to get off. The man that seals the cars opened the door and seen us; if he had not seen us I don't know what would have happened to us up in there for we had no water and the car was to go through to Mexico . We stayed in Del Rio until the next morning and got the local at 6:30, but the conductor made us get off at Comstock, Tex. As nothing stops there we walked three miles to where they were grading as all the trains had to slow up. So we caught another freight and rode the bumpers to Pecos Viaduct. We stayed there half a day and all night and walked to Shulma the next morning; we were very tired and dirty. There was only two white men there, the rest Mexicans, but they treated us very nice, they gave us something to eat and we slept in the station house.*

We remained there three days when we got a local to Sanderson, but the Conductor seen us and we had to get off there. So we stayed in

Sanderson two days looking for work, but there was no work there, so we got a freight at four o'clock in the morning out of there and came to Alpine. I worked about a week and my pal wanted to get to El Paso so I quit work and rode the blind of the passenger to Valtine, where the porter made us get off. We stayed there until the next day and got a freight out in the afternoon. The brakeman seen us but said he would not make us get off. We were in a coal car loaded with lumber. There was just enough room for us to sit down. It was terrible warm, but we could not stand up for fear the conductor would see us and make us get off. We arrived at El Paso at 10:30 at night, very tired dirty and hungry. We went to the El Paso Hotel got a room and bath and stayed until the next day. I went to work and my pal is going to Alpine to get married to a railroad man she met on the coming over here. The trip was not so hard, but it was dangerous and tiresome. This is a true story and each place I have mentioned you can inquire and they will tell you that an Irish girl and a Mexican girl beat their way through there. I would give you my pal's name, but she is going to get married. Her husband might not like it."

Watoga Bouidnot

Wilcox, Arizona

American postcard c-1910

# City of Bisbee Ordinance No. 4 February 1902
# (Only parts that affect red-light district)

**Section 1.** If any person shall appear in any place within this town of Bisbee in a state of nudity, in a dress not belonging to his or her sex or in any indecent or lewd dress, or shall make any indecent exposure of his or her person, or be guilty of any lewd indecent act or behavior, or shall expose sell or offer any indecent or lewd book, picture or other things, or shall exhibit or perform any indecent, immoral or lewd play or other representation every such person shall be deemed guilty of a misdemeanor and upon conviction there of shall be fined three hundred dollars, or be imprisoned in the town or county jail for a period not exceeding three months, or be punished by both such fine and imprisonment

**Section 3.** Any prostitute, courtesan or lewd woman who shall, within the city limits of the town, by word, sign or action ply her vocation upon the streets or at any place or at any door or open window of a house or room she may occupy, or make any public or meretricious display of herself of herself upon the streets or in any public place, shall be deemed guilty of a misdemeanor and upon conviction thereof, shall be fined in any sum not exceeding fifty dollars or imprisoned in the town or county jail for any period of time not exceeding one month or punished by both such fine and imprisonment.

**Section 14.** If any saloon, gambling house, house of prostitution, dance house keeper or proprietor of any agents or clerks of any such proprietors or keepers shall sell or permit to be sold, in his or her or their place of business, to any minor, any such liquors, he she, or they shall be deemed guilty of a misdemeanor and upon conviction thereof, shall be fined in any sum not exceeding fifty dollars or imprisoned in the town or county jail for any period of time not exceeding one month or punished by both such fine and imprisonment.

**Section 15.** Any minor who shall be found in any billiard hall. Barroom, bowling alley house of ill-fame, or place where obscene plays are performed within the limits of the town, between the hours of nine o'clock in the evening and six o'clock in the morning, unless able to give a lawful excuse

therefore, or who shall frequent or be found in any saloon, billiard hall, house of ill-fame, bowling alley or place where obscene plays are performed, participating in any game or drinking intoxicating or malt liquors shall be deemed guilty of a misdemeanor and upon conviction thereof, shall be fined in any sum not exceeding fifty dollars or imprisoned in the town or county jail for any period of time not exceeding one month or punished by both such fine and imprisonment.

French postcard c-1908

# Bibliography

"$600 in Jewelry is Recovered; Stones Found in his Shoe" Bisbee Daily Review 27, March 1914 page 5
"2 Captured in Naco; Hunt Continues" Bisbee Daily Review 24, February 1914 page 1
"2 Captured in Naco" Bisbee Daily Review 24, February 1914 page 3
"Another Killing" Cochise Review 26, January 1901 page 2
"Arrest May Follow" Bisbee Daily Review 1, October 1908 page 7
"Arrest Pesquiera" Bisbee Daily Review 24, April 1920 page 2
"Arrested for Insanity" Bisbee Daily Review 28, May 1912 page 4
"Arrested on Serious Charge" Bisbee Daily Review 25, October 1904 page 1
"Arrested on Suspicion" Bisbee Daily Review 10, September1903 page 5
"Beats his Wife in Brutal Manner" Bisbee Daily Review 27, February 1904 page 5
Bell, Ernest Albert. Fighting the Traffic in Young Girls. N.p.: n.p., 1910. Print.
"Bisbee Courts Grind out Grist" Bisbee Daily Review 8 September 1909 page 1
"Bisbee is on Trial" Bisbee Daily Review 1, March 1904 page 4
"Bisbee Jottings" Tombstone Epitaph 14, May 1899 page 2
"Bisbee Jottings" Tombstone Epitaph 9, July 1899 page 1
"Bisbee Prisoner out on October 27" Bisbee Daily Review 22, October 1908 page 5
"Blood Suckers Should Go" Bisbee Daily Review 28, February 1904 page 4
"Bound Over to Await Action of Grand Jury" Bisbee Daily Review 1, May1907 page 8
"Brewery Gulch is Damaged by Storm" Bisbee Daily Review 14, August 1917 page 3
"Brewery Gulch Suffers Heavy Damaged by Storm" Bisbee Daily Review 14, August 1917 page 1
"Card of Thanks" Bisbee Daily Review 24, July 1908 page 7
"Case Against Women Dismissed" Bisbee Daily Review 18, August 1903 page 5
"Change of Venue in Tenderloin Case" Bisbee Daily Review 2, June 1906 page 6
Chisholm, Joe. Brewery Gulch: Frontier Days of Old Arizona, Last Outpost of the Great Southwest. San Antonio, TX: Naylor, 1949. Print.
"City Council Meeting" Bisbee Daily Review 6, December,1903 page 4
"Classified Ads" Bisbee Daily Review 5, June 1904 page 6
"Closed Up" Bisbee Daily Review 11, December 1917 page 8
"Cochise County Coroner's Inquest #1200" Arizona State Archives Phoenix
"Cochise County Coroner's Inquest #244" Arizona State Archives Phoenix
"Cochise County Coroner's Inquest #4" Arizona State Archives Phoenix
"Cochise County Coroner's Inquest #437" Arizona State Archives Phoenix
"Cochise County Coroner's Inquest #596" Arizona State Archives Phoenix
"Cochise County Coroner's Inquest #9" Arizona State Archives Phoenix
"Cochise County Coroner's Inquest of Rosario Tapeta, December 18, 1900" Arizona State Archives Phoenix
"Cochise County" The Oasis 24, June189 9page 5
"Con Shea Convicted" Bisbee Daily Review 2, March 1904 page 4
"Copperings" Tombstone Epitaph 21, May 1899 page 1
"Cora Miles Arrested" Bisbee Daily Review 11, August 1903 page 5
"Cora Miles Dismissed" Bisbee Daily Review 16, August 1903 page 5
"County Recorders Recent Work" Tombstone Epitaph 8, December 1901 page 4
"Court Hears Mabry Case and Finds Woman Guilty" Bisbee Daily Review 14, December 1909 page 8
"Courtroom Looks Like House Party" Bisbee Daily Review 23, December 1909 page 3
"Cut with Water Pitcher" Bisbee Daily Review 24, March 1902 page 1

"Dairyman is Fined $50 in City Court After Many Delays" <u>Bisbee Daily Review</u> 4, April 1917 page 5
"Drastic Laws for Restricted Area to Be Enforced" <u>Bisbee Daily Review</u> 14, November 1914 page 3
"Dunbar Case Before High Judge." <u>Bisbee Daily Review</u> 15, June 1911 page 5
"Dunbar's Jaw Broken by Rough" <u>Bisbee Daily Review</u> 9, August 1906 page 8
"Embezzlement Cases Dismissed" <u>Bisbee Daily Review</u> 29, April 1904 page 5
"Evasions of Wine Room Ordinance" <u>Bisbee Daily Review</u> 6, August 1905 page 8
"False Report" <u>Bisbee Daily Review</u> 9, December 1905 page 2
"Fight Startles All Lowell Saturday" <u>Bisbee Daily Review</u> 19, July 1910 page 8
"Fined $20 for Assault" <u>Bisbee Daily Review</u> 23, November 1905 page 4
"Fined $5 Each" <u>Bisbee Daily Review</u> 25, March 1902 page 8
"First Case Under "White Slave Act" Shows Law's Reach" <u>Bisbee Daily Review</u> 31, March 1911 page 8
"For White Slavery" <u>Bisbee Daily Review</u> 19, May 1921 page 6
"Forfeited Bail." <u>Bisbee Daily Review</u> 6, June 1917 page 6
"From Tuesday's Daily" <u>Tombstone Epitaph</u> 22, August 1909 page 3
"Girls Arrests Leads to Probe by U.S. Agents." <u>Bisbee Daily Review</u> 28, March 1922 page 8
"Girls Tell Story of Revolting Crime and Carousals" <u>Bisbee Daily Review</u> 10, December 1909 page 1
"Girls Tell Story of Revolting Crime" <u>Bisbee Daily Review</u> 10, December 1909 page 8
"Harnessmaker gets it Tangle" <u>Bisbee Daily Review</u> 18, December 1909 page 8
"Hate and Disorder in the Tenderloin" <u>Bisbee Daily Review</u> 7, May 1911 page 8
"Heavy Fine is Given Tenderloin Artist" <u>Bisbee Daily Review</u> 28, March 1911 page 8
"Hold-up and Murder is Committed in Heart of City" <u>Bisbee Daily Review</u> 19, August 1903 page 1
"Hold-up and Murder is Committed in Heart of City" <u>Bisbee Daily Review</u> 19, August 1903 page 8
"Hold-up Men May Yet Get It" <u>Bisbee Daily Review</u> 2, January 1906 page 8
"Hop Joint Case is Dismissed" <u>Bisbee Daily Review</u> 5, September 1903 page 5
"Hop Layout Found in House of Ill-Fame" <u>Bisbee Daily Review</u> 4, September 1903 page 1
"House on School Hill Holds Girls as Prisoners" <u>Bisbee Daily Review</u> 11, December 1909 page 1
"In the Justice Court" <u>Bisbee Daily Review</u> 25, March 1909 page 2
"Indians on Big Time" "<u>Bisbee Daily Review</u> 28, September 1915 page 8
"Insane Woman Attempts Suicide" <u>Bisbee Daily Review</u> 17, November 1905 page 8
"Irene Logan Killed" <u>Graham Guardian</u> 19. May 1899 page 4
"It is A Felonious Charge" <u>Bisbee Daily Review</u> 15, August 1903 page 5
"Jail Break is Foiled Two Times" <u>Bisbee Daily Review</u> 29, March 1914 page 1
"Jealous Woman Goes After Husband and Tries to Kill Him" <u>Bisbee Daily Review</u> 15, June 1911 page 8
"Jewelry Valued at $2,000 is Stolen" <u>Bisbee Daily Review</u> 8, May 1917 page 2
"Judgement Rendered "<u>Bisbee Daily Review</u> 6, October 1904 page 5
"Justice Court Work in City" <u>Bisbee Daily Review</u> 21, June 1905 page 5
Kane, H. H. Opium-smoking in America and China: A Study of Its Prevalence, and Effects, Immediate and Remote, on the Individual and the Nation. New York: G.P. Putnam's Sons, 1882. Print.
"Lads in Justice Court" <u>Bisbee Daily Review</u> 27, December 1905 page 5
"Last Round in Fight" <u>Bisbee Daily Review</u> 6, August 1903 page 5
"Lowell Morality Move" <u>Bisbee Daily Review</u> 21, February 1905 page 5
"Lowell Pistol Wielder Said to be in Bisbee" <u>Bisbee Daily Review</u> 24, April 1906 page 5
"Main St. Petition has Ben Amended" <u>Bisbee Daily Review</u> 23, September 1905 page 5

"Man Possibly Fatally Hurt in a Disreputable House" Bisbee Daily Review 6, February1906 page 3
"Masked Men Hold up Con Shea's Saloon" Weekly Arizona Journal-Miner 3, January 1906 page 2
"Miller is Bound Over in Sum of $500" Bisbee Daily Review 11, August 1906 page 8
"Miller is Bound Over in Sum of $500" Bisbee Daily Review 11, August 1906 page 8
"Miller's Bondsmen Will Have to Pay up" Bisbee Daily Review 23, December 1911 page 6
 Miner, Maude E. Slavery of Prostitution: A Plea for Emancipation. New York: Macmilan, 1916. Print.
"Miss Sharp Fined" Bisbee Daily Review 25, February1917 page 8
"More Trouble for Council" Bisbee Daily Review 17, January 1906 page 5
"More Trouble Had" Bisbee Daily Review 7, March 1916 page 6
"Mrs. Chaffin gets Divorce Decree" Bisbee Daily Review 18, July 1911 page 8
"Mrs. Thos Fox is Found Guilty" Bisbee Daily Review 20 June 1905 page 5
"Naco Bull fights" Bisbee Daily Review 27, December 1901 page 1
"Naked Woman Creates Excitement at Warren" Bisbee Daily Review 24, April 1907 page 8
"Negro Trooper is Killed, Protecting Woman in Robbery" Bisbee Daily Review 14, March 1916 page 5
"No More Dope" Bisbee Daily Review 16, December 1909 page 7
"No Room in City for These" Bisbee Daily Review 7, March 1913 page 3
"No. 41 Proves Trap for Girl" Bisbee Daily Review 19, December 1909 page 1
"Nofts was Not Stabbed" Bisbee Daily Review 19, August 1903 page 5
"Officers Have in Custody Supposed Murders" Bisbee Daily Review 1, October 1903 page 4
"Officers Have in Custody, Men Supposed to have Murdered L.O. Milless" Bisbee Daily Review 1, October 1903 page 1
"Officers Raid Joint and Capture Opium Layout and Smokers" Bisbee Daily Review 19, October 1916 page 3
"Officers Stop Hilarity" Bisbee Daily Review 16, June 1907 page 5
"Official Report" Tombstone Epitaph 10, April 1892 page 3
"Ordinance 81" Bisbee Daily Review 7, January 1906 page 8
"Ordinance 81" Bisbee Daily Review 9, January 1906 page 6
"Ordinance 95" Bisbee Daily Review 16 June 1906 page 7
"Ordinance No.18" Bisbee Daily Review 11, July 1902 page 7
"Ordinance No.4" Bisbee Daily Review 4, February 1902 page 3
"Ordinance No.4" Bisbee Daily Review 9, February 1902 page 3
"Ordinance No.79" Bisbee Daily Review 12, December 1905 page 3
"Original Certificate of Death." Arizona Department of Health Services http://genealogy.az.gov/azdeath/011/10111861.pdf. (October 15, 2016)
"Parker Woman is Freed by Court" Bisbee Daily Review 18, June 1911 page 8
"Proceedings at Tombstone Court" Bisbee Daily Review 24, May 1911 page 8
"Raid House that is Near a School" Bisbee Daily Review 23, April 1912 page 8
"Raid Many Resorts; Arrest Nine Persons" Bisbee Daily Review 6, December 1910 page 8
"Raided House" Bisbee Daily Review 16, April 1918 page 5
"Raids in Order" Bisbee Daily Review 18, April 1906 page 7
"Raising a Rough house" Bisbee Daily Review 29, November 1903 page 5
"Record goes Smash with Conviction of Douglas Bootlegger" Bisbee Daily Review 17, August 1916 page 5
"Red Light District May Be Closed Up" Bisbee Daily Review 2, December 1917 page 8
"Red Light District of Bisbee Must Go City Fathers Say" Bisbee Daily Review 5, December 1917 page 3
"Red Lighters Invade Lowell" Bisbee Daily Review 28, June 1905 page 5
"Redlight Mixup is Finally Settled" Bisbee Daily Review 11, September1909 page 1
"Restricted District Closed" Weekly-Journal Miner11, December 1912 page 6
"Ritner rearrested" Bisbee Daily Review 30, April 1912 page 8
"Robbery in Tenderloin" Bisbee Daily Review 1, August 1903 page 5

Roe, Clifford G. The Great War on White Slavery. N.p.: Private, 1911. Print.
"Savage Attempt to Murder is Charged" Bisbee Daily Review 28, April 1907 page 5
"Sentenced to Prison" Bisbee Daily Review 22, November 1916 page 8
"Sentence is Moderate" Bisbee Daily Review 7, August 1912 page 2
"Sheriff's Certificate of Sale" Tombstone Epitaph 26, March 1911 page 3
"Shooting Case to be Brought up Today" Bisbee Daily Review 17, June 1911 page 8
"Shooting Scrape Cost One Liberty and Other His Arm" Bisbee Daily Review 22, February 1914 page 1
"Soldiers Barred from Restricted Douglas District" Bisbee Daily Review 14, March 1916 page 3
"Stabbed by Wife" Bisbee Daily Review 16, December 1904 page 1
"Suspects Say They're Not Guilty" Bisbee Daily Review 25, December 1904 page 5
"Swallowed Carbolic Acid" Bisbee Daily Review 22, September 1905 page 8
Swift, Morrison I. Prostitution, a Remedy: Bills and Petitions Presented to the Massachusetts Legislature in the Session of 1911-12. Boston: Liberty, 1912. Print.
"Take Desperado and Woman on Federal Charge, After Urgent Washington Wire. Bisbee Daily Review 13, February 1914 page 1
"Taken to Hospital" Bisbee Daily Review 15, January, 1910 page 8
"Tenderloin Amazons Break Speed Ordinance" Bisbee Daily Review 10, July, 1906 page 1
"Tenderloin Fight" Bisbee Daily Review 27, April 1912 page 3
"The Blackmail Law" Bisbee Daily Review 26, September 1916 page 4
"The Case Fell Down" Arizona Republican 6, May 1906 page 4
"Thieves Taken by Officers in Hot Pursuit" Bisbee Daily Review 26, March 1914 page 3
"To Get Cigar Bill" Bisbee Daily Review 3, September 1903 page 5
"To Whom it May Concern" Bisbee Daily Review 12, March 1911 page 6
"Tough Tenderloin is Hailed into Court" Bisbee Daily Review 14, March 1912 page 6
"Tries to Cut Throat of Guest" Bisbee Daily Review 6, June 1911 page 8
"Tries to Shoot Paramour and Gets 90 Days Bisbee Daily Review 6, August 1912 page 4
"Tucson Scandalized by Modern Dress- Pretty Actress Says Bisbee Didn't Mind It- Below are the Girl and the Garb" Bisbee Daily Review 7, September 1913 page 5
"Two are Arrested" Bisbee Daily Review 18, May 1918 page 6
"Two Break Jail Early in Morning" Bisbee Daily Review 22, February 1914 page 1
"Two Women Charged with Having Booze" Bisbee Daily Review 1, June 1917 page 5
"Unknown Man Commits Suicide by Rope Route" Bisbee Daily Review 15, January 1910 page 8
"Untitled" Bisbee Daily Review 3, March 1904 page 4
"Untitled" Bisbee Daily Review 11, August 1905 page 6
"Untitled" Cochise Review 26, January 1901 page 3
"Untitled" Cochise Review 29, December 1900 page 4
"Untitled" The Arizona Daily Orb 11, January 1900 page 4
"Untitled" The Weekly Orb 18, June 1899 page 2
"Valuable Jewel is Returned Through Effort of Officers"" Bisbee Daily Review 10, August 1915 page 8
"Verdict Guilty is Found" Bisbee Daily Review 17, April 1918 page 3
"Violation of Mann Act Charged Here" Bisbee Daily Review 4, February 1916 page 1
"Wages of Women" Bisbee Daily Review 11 March 1913 page 4
"Warren Dry Now and for All Time Despite Election" Bisbee Daily Review 23, November 1909 page 8
"Was Discharged" Bisbee Daily Review 17, January 1903 page 8
"Water Rate for Sewer" Bisbee Daily Review 23, December 1905 page 1
"White Slave Case" Bisbee Daily Review 25, March 1911 page 7
"White Slavery Case on Trial" Bisbee Daily Review 26, August 1913 page 5
"White Slaving Charge Made" Bisbee Daily Review 8, August 1913 page 8
"Who Threw that Rock" Bisbee Daily Review 16, January 1903 page 8
"Wild Ride is Costly" Bisbee Daily Review 24, August 1910 page 5

"Will Deport Woman" Bisbee Daily Review 12, April 1910 page 5
"Williams Going After Cities Which Collect Licenses" Bisbee Daily Review 3, October, 1909 page 1

"Woman Beater Again in Toils" Bisbee Daily Review 28, February 1904 page 5
"Woman Charges Husband in Brutal Attack" Tombstone Epitaph 1, February 1920 page 5
"Woman is Heavily Fined for Fight" Bisbee Daily Review 28, October 1909 page 8
"Woman Paraded Streets Naked" Bisbee Daily Review 29, June 1905 page 5
"Women are in Jail" Bisbee Daily Review 16, August 1903 page 5
"Women Pull Hair Then Pay Fine" Bisbee Daily Review 17, December 1909 page 8
"Would Marry French Girl to Save Her" Bisbee Daily Review 12, July 1908 page 5
"Writes Story of Hobo Life and Suicides" Bisbee Daily Review 6, December 1910 page 8

## LOWELL PISTOL WIELDER SAID TO BE IN BISBEE.

The young man who is alleged to have married a young woman and then put her in a house of ill-fame, and she not supplying him with the amount of money called for by him, beat her over the head with a revolver in a saloon at Lowell the other night, is said to be in Bisbee. It was stated after the fracas that he had departed for parts unknown, but the officers believe that he is still in this city. Whether or not his arrest will follow is not known.

Bisbee Daily Review April 1906

French postcard c-1908

www.ingramcontent.com/pod-product-compliance
Lightning Source LLC
Chambersburg PA
CBHW071310110426
42743CB00042B/1246